"Isaiah teaches how and why your habits, behaviors and values are at the core of performance or lack thereof. He doesn't sugarcoat anything so there aren't any wasted words or pages in any of his publications. This book just went to the top of my must read twice list."

—**Craig Morantz, Former CEO of Kira Talent and Founder of Vegan Labs**

"*The Science of Intelligent Achievement* was a blessing and a curse. It was a blessing because the book showed me how to be aware of the thing that I do on a daily basis that waste my mental energy. You really don't realize how much energy you freely give away to people and situations that don't matter. Isaiah says repeatedly that busyness is not productivity and he is right. The book was a curse because it completely demolished all of my excuses and made me start taking responsibility for my decisions again."

—**Josh Birt, Video Producer for Twitter and Founder of Josh Birt Productions**

"*The Science of Intelligent Achievement* is well researched and provides an excellent blueprint to real success. Every page is loaded with sage advice and you will find yourself savoring every morsel of it. You will learn how to live the life of your dreams by eliminating negative people, thoughts, and things that drain your mental energy. Stop being busy, develop focus, get rid of distractions, and master the art of effectiveness by using the free tools Isaiah provides here."

—**Linda Mitchell, IIN Health Coach, ADP Holistic Health Practitioner and CEO The ChickFit Studio**

"The key ⟨…⟩ of lear⟨…⟩ ⟨…⟩rning how to learn. How to achieve peak performance in a difficult arena of life that requires mastering 100 micro-skills to become among the best in that field. Isaiah Hankel breaks down that meta-language, and shows us how, regardless of our life's mission, to quickly achieve mastery in whatever field of life inspires us."

—**James Altucher, Journalist and Author of** *Choose Yourself*

"The biggest advantage of reading *The Science of Intelligent Achievement* is the sense of personal responsibility the book provides. Most books in this category are either pure fluff in that they offer nothing but feel good nonsense about how to 'be grateful' and 'be nice', or they are written with the goal of absolving the reader or any fault in life. Here, Isaiah takes a completely different angle as he puts the responsibility of choosing your focus, creating something worthwhile in life, and continuing to grow pragmatically squarely on the reader's shoulders. Every page pushes you to take control rather than give up control, to actively choose what to spend your mental energy on rather than just 'letting go' and hoping for the best. It's a great read if you're up for the challenge of taking ownership over the good and bad in your life."

—**Jordan Harbinger, Co-Founder of The Art of Charm and Sirius Radio Talk Show Host**

"*The Science of Intelligent Achievement* unapologetically slapped me in the face by telling me what common mistakes 'average' people do and how these 'average' habits and actions are keeping me in a mediocre career and life. There is something fresh and simple about Isaiah's ability to not sugar-coat topics. This books is full of relatable stories and interesting facts that stay with you after you are done reading. I recommend this tough-as-nails self-help book to anyone who wants to evaluate their direction in life."

—**Dr. Nick Ross, Senior R&D Engineer at Intel**

"This is a jam-packed book that is chock-full of actionable and practical advice on the hard truth about what it takes to live a happy and successful life. You won't be able to make excuses for yourself after reading this book."

—**Ben Greenfield, Founder of Greenfield Fitness Systems** ⟨…⟩trition

"Is there anything more boring than traditional self-help books? Thankfully Isaiah has written something untraditional here. *The Science of Intelligent Achievement* digs beneath the surface of what make measurable growth possible – identifying the patterns, processes and science behind being successful in any field. He does all of this while infusing each chapter with real-world examples, humor, and a much-needed dose of personal responsibility and hard truth."

—Anthony DiMarco, Entrepreneurs' Organization Global Trainer and CEO of the DiMarco Group

"*The Science of Intelligent Achievement* showed me how to take ownership of my life and how to organize and prioritize myself both professionally and personally. Make no mistake, the book is hard hitting and makes you face yourself head on. Each chapter practically forces you to start implementing positive and pragmatic changes. The book shows you that it's never too late to turn things around as long as you're willing to take personal responsibility for where you are in life."

—Dr. Klodjan Stafa, Senior Scientist at Estée Lauder Companies

"Reading this book is like a healthy punch in the gut. Many of us 'top performers' present externally as having it all when, really, we're miserable inside chasing after someone else's version of success. Isaiah's gripping personal story is a harbinger of what can happen if you fail to listen to the voice inside reminding you of who you really are. His framework of selectivity, ownership and pragmatism is one I wished I had when I was going through a similar time. If you're ready to reclaim your life, live it according to your own standards, and take back control, you need this book. I dare you to read it and not come out transformed."

—Margo Aaron, Former Strategic Planner at Hunter Straker, Founder of That Seems Important

"Isaiah has created a brilliant, practical, goal-oriented, scientifically-backed, self-improvement book, suitable for anyone struggling to make the next step in their life or career. His new book has already been pivotal for me in harnessing my mental energy and focus to drive my career forward."

—Dr. Yousuf Ali, Medical Science Liaison at Novartis

The Science of Intelligent Achievement

The Science
of Intelligent
Achievement

How Smart People Focus,
Create and Grow
Their Way to Success

Isaiah Hankel

CAPSTONE
A Wiley Brand

Registered office

John Wiley & Sons Ltd, The Atrium, Southern Gate, Chichester, West Sussex, PO19 8SQ, United Kingdom.

For details of our global editorial offices, for customer services and for information about how to apply for permission to reuse the copyright material in this book please see our website at www.wiley.com.

Wiley publishes in a variety of print and electronic formats and by print-on-demand. Some material included with standard print versions of this book may not be included in e-books or in print-on-demand. If this book refers to media such as a CD or DVD that is not included in the version you purchased, you may download this material at http://booksupport.wiley.com. For more information about Wiley products, visit www.wiley.com.

Designations used by companies to distinguish their products are often claimed as trademarks. All brand names and product names used in this book are trade names, service marks, trademarks or registered trademarks of their respective owners. The publisher is not associated with any product or vendor mentioned in this book.

Limit of Liability/Disclaimer of Warranty: While the publisher and author have used their best efforts in preparing this book, they make no representations or warranties with respect to the accuracy or completeness of the contents of this book and specifically disclaim any implied warranties of merchantability or fitness for a particular purpose. It is sold on the understanding that the publisher is not engaged in rendering professional services and neither the publisher nor the author shall be liable for damages arising herefrom. If professional advice or other expert assistance is required, the services of a competent professional should be sought.

Library of Congress Cataloging-in-Publication Data is Available:

ISBN 978–0–857–08760–7 (paperback)
ISBN 978–0–857–08770–6 (ePDF)
ISBN 978–0–857–08772–0 (ePub)

Cover Design: Wiley
Cover Image: © Lava 4 images/Shutterstock

Set in 12/16pt AGaramondPro by SPi Global, Chennai, India

Printed in Great Britain by TJ International Ltd, Padstow, Cornwall, UK

10 9 8 7 6 5 4 3 2 1

To my wife, Laura, and daughter, Zara

CONTENTS

FOREWORD

Twenty years ago I left my hometown. Recently, I found myself back there. Unfortunately, I was there for my Grandpap's funeral. He was a patriarch, a war hero, and a role model for each member of our family. He had left a legacy behind by living with authenticity.

While reconnecting with siblings and greeting friends of the family, I was struck by how much I'd grown since I left town. I had been the first in our family to graduate college. I got married, I enrolled in graduate school, had a child, received a Ph.D., trained at the National Institutes of Health, and landed a dream job at Harvard Medical School (HMS). However, my path hasn't been easy.

In the beginning, I worked hard, but I didn't work smart.

I was out of focus. I wasn't living in reality. I hadn't taken full responsibility for my choices. I wasn't being strategic ... and I definitely wasn't being authentic.

It wasn't until I had a frank and honest conversation about how I could leverage my experience and my interests to do something fulfilling and to start achieving intelligently. It was then that everything came into focus, I faced a harsh reality and took responsibility for my life and my career.

My journey is far from complete. And I do not go alone. In addition to my indomitable wife, I've had a few close friends and colleagues help me along the way. And of course I've returned the favor. When one of these friends asked me to write the foreword to his second book, I had to help him out and said yes immediately.

Isaiah and I first met via an email introduction. He had a novel approach to leadership and career development so I invited him to give a talk at HMS. Through several conversations and a growing friendship Isaiah was open to my advice, and criticisms. While my opinions were plentiful, he shrewdly picked up on the important points and began to craft his message and share it across the globe. I invited him back to HMS two more times, once for a Leadership Series and another for his Career Development workshops. In turn, he's twice invited me to appear on his webinar series where my aim was to empower professionals to confidently (and scientifically) take control of their career and lives.

In Isaiah's second book, *The Science of Intelligent Achievement*, he tackles some issues that apply to most everyone: focus, creative ownership, and pragmatic growth. When Isaiah brings up "Blind Spot Ignorance" in Chapter 29, he discusses how we can identify blind spots in others but not usually ourselves. He also states that self-perception rarely matches social perception. To combat this Blind Spot Ignorance, Isaiah advises to keep blind your spots in full view. This requires a fearless self-inventory where you take ownership of your shortcomings, mistakes, and biases. Once you self-monitor for bad habits and potential pitfalls, you will no longer be "blindsided" by the truth and can begin to live with authenticity.

Selective investment of your focus, energy, and relationships; taking creative ownership of your path, success, and happiness; and a pragmatic approach to your decisions, habits, and overall growth will lead you towards your authentic self. And it's this kind of achievement that will result in increased productivity, a meaningful message, and a lasting legacy in your life.

I wish I had this book twenty years ago because to me, *Intelligent Achievement* starts and ends with authenticity, or as Isaiah calls it in this book "true success."

—James Gould, Ph.D.,
Director, Office for Postdoctoral Fellows,
Harvard Medical School

PREFACE: A FOOL'S GUIDE TO FAKE SUCCESS

No man, for any considerable period, can wear one face to himself and another to the multitude, without finally getting bewildered as to which may be the true.

—Nathaniel Hawthorne

My real doctor was on vacation. This new doctor was merely stepping in to examine me as part of a routine annual physical. By chance, the new doctor was older, much more experienced, and had just diagnosed two other male patients with testicular tumors.

It was as if he was *primed* to diagnose me as well.

After noticing my right testicle was slightly smaller than my left, the doctor ordered a series of labs to confirm that I indeed had a tumor. What followed was the most life-altering, life-changing, terrifying experience I've ever had.

I was called in to have an ultrasound and, as the technician examined me, I could see the results in her eyes. I asked her sporadic questions and she gently dodged them with some "I don't knows" punctuated with a "we have to wait for the results from the radiologist." *Just like she's been trained to do for all the other people having biopsies and waiting on their death sentences*, I thought.

My heart pounded harder and harder each time she avoided the obvious answer.

The doctor who performed the initial exams called me at eight o'clock the next morning to confirm that there was a mass in my right testicle and it had to be removed *immediately*.

As you might know from your own personal trials, news like this squeezes and twists your heart.

I was angry, sad, and lost. I walked around the city in a daze, and all the smiling people seemed so far from me. I was alone in this.

A few hours later, my surgery was scheduled … a few hours more and I was under the knife.

The Carefully Crafted Veil is Lifted

I woke up from the surgery, hungry and wonky from the drugs.

But hunger quickly turned into exhaustion. I was completely drained from worry and the trauma of surgery. Just as I got home and flopped down on the bed, weak and depressed, the urologist called me.

My heart jumped into my throat. The squeezing and twisting started again.

"Hello?" I whispered.

"Good news, Isaiah. The imaging results just came back and nothing has spread. I thought you'd want to know that before bed."

Thank you, God. Thank you, God. Thank you, God, Jesus, and all the angels, I thought.

I spent the next two weeks avoiding reality in more ways than one. Pain meds. TV binges. Pizza deliveries. My normal life full of responsibilities, work, errands, and things to do seemed to drift away, forgotten.

The pain meds ran out just as I was just getting used to my new comatose lifestyle.

Hello, reality. Hello, strange new world.

Nothing felt familiar. I was in unknown territory.

Something had changed in me. Something significant.

Who was I supposed to be now?

Slowly, the carefully crafted veil I had manufactured throughout the years—you know, all those illusions we design to shield us from the truth of our lives and the baser nature of ourselves—lifted, and I could see my life as it really was with stark clarity.

Not the life that I was pretending to live.

Not the life that I had shown to other people at work or on Facebook.

Not the life that I had projected for so long that I had come to believe it was real.

My actual, authentic, ugly life.

I slowly realized that I had spent years chasing after illusions, following a fool's guide to fake success. And as for my achievements in this pursuit, what were they really? Everything that made me "me" now seemed as lasting and meaningful as a sandcastle on the shore's edge. None of it *mattered*.

The surface nature of all my relationships was suddenly glaringly obvious. That's what immediately stood out. I didn't like or admire any of my so-called friends. *My life is a lie in so many ways*, I thought.

Then, I saw the falsity—the mocking joke of my chosen career path.

This is not me, this job, I thought. This isn't what I want or am meant to do with my life.

My "healthy lifestyle" was laughable. How healthy could a fake life be? How much was I depleting my health and energy to live a lie?

My fake personality. My fake identity.

One after another, all the falsities and pretenses of my life were parading before me.

What a fraud I had become. No, worse, I was a *disaster*.

My relationships were a disaster. Half of them had faded into the background of my life and the other half were completely fake to begin with. Connections that had once been built on shared values and tied together tightly with meaning, were now frayed, loose, and superficial.

I was no longer selective with who I gave my time and energy to. Instead, I had become completely passive, allowing anything and anyone into my life.

My career was a disaster. I thought I had achieved an untouchable job title. I thought I had become irreplaceable. In reality, my employer was ready to cut me loose after three weeks of medical leave. I was completely dependent on them for my survival. I owned nothing and owed everything.

My health, which I once touted as Olympic-level when I was a NCAA Division I wrestler at University, was now average at best, thanks to an undisciplined diet and "just a couple of beers with the guys" every night.

I stopped being reasonable and pragmatic, choosing instead to live life with my head in the clouds. I chose to evade reality. I avoided even the slightest attachment to personal responsibility because surely someone else was watching out for me. Surely, there were no real consequences to this life and even if there were, I could turn everything around at a moment's notice if I really wanted to.

Within two months of my surgery, I went from feeling on top of the world to realizing that I was just a few weeks away from being broke ... and that I was completely alone, completely out of touch with reality, and soon to be remembered only as a cautionary tale.

From Tragedy to Intelligent Achievement

Tragedy, while painful, is enlightening.

Tragedy is an opportunity for growth.

When I found out the news that I needed surgery, the first thing that jumped in my head was, "This can't be happening."

Now, I'm thankful that it did. The diagnosis changed my life for the better. It showed me how foolish I had been, chasing after fake signals of achievement. Cancer showed me everything that I had wasted and taught me that it was time for me to do a hard reevaluation of my life.

It didn't happen overnight. Nothing good does.

Slowly, I learned where I needed to stop spending my energy and where to start *investing* my energy instead.

Over the course of the next year, I stopped following my fool's guide to fake success. I stopped wasting time on things like my "image," job title, salary, and—especially—the next good time.

Instead, I started *selectively focusing* my energy in new, positive people and pursuits. I stopped allowing myself to be dependent on others and instead took *creative ownership* over my own success and happiness. I also decided to get back in touch with reality. I decided to start exercising *pragmatic growth*—to see things for how they are, not just how I wanted them to be.

Together, these three things—selectivity, ownership, and pragmatism—came together to form a kind of guidepost for me; one that directed me toward *The Science of Intelligent Achievement*, instead of fake success.

Now, thanks to this guidepost, I'm married to my best friend, I run two companies with close friends and colleagues—companies that help hundreds of thousands of people and are truly successful in terms of both profits and cash-flow—and just welcomed my first kid into the world.

Enter this book.

I wrote *The Science of Intelligent Achievement* to show you how to create your own guidepost of selectivity, ownership, and pragmatism; and in part as a cautionary tale, to help you avoid the common mistake of chasing after fake success like I did.

My hope is that the pages that follow will lead you to the highest levels of Intelligent Achievement in your own life.

ACKNOWLEDGMENTS

This book is for everyone who helped me *achieve real success through selective focus, creative ownership, and pragmatic growth.* Hard lessons and incredible people made this possible.

To my family, including my wife and daughter, Laura and Zara, who have filled my life with many *intelligent adventures.* To my parents, John and Karen, and my brother and sister, Noah and Jessica, for teaching me the importance of *taking ownership over my life* and for always reminding me to be *selective with my mental energy.*

To Team Cheeky, including all of my friends and colleagues at Cheeky Scientist for helping me make a *pragmatic* difference in the world. Thank you for working so hard to *turn our message, "Remember your value as a PhD" into a magnet.*

To all the members of the Cheeky Scientist Association for continually striving to improve their lives and improve the world. You are all an example of *seeing through the victim illusion* and *turning pain into productivity.*

To everyone who has ever supported or spoken well of Hankel Leadership, including members of *My Life Aligned.* You have set the standard for the *law of relaxed productivity.*

Keep *avoiding willpower depletion* and keep *hacking and stacking mini-habits to success.*

To Annie, Chloe, Pete, and everyone at Wiley for believing in this book and helping me bring it to life.

ABOUT THE AUTHOR

 Isaiah Hankel received his doctorate in Anatomy and Cell Biology and is an expert on mental focus, behavioral psychology, and career development. His work has been featured in *The Guardian*, *Fast Company*, and *Entrepreneur Magazine*. Isaiah's previous book, *Black Hole Focus*, was published by Wiley, and was selected as Business Book of the Month in the U.K., and became a business bestseller internationally. Isaiah has delivered corporate presentations to over 20,000 people, including over 300 workshops and keynotes worldwide in the past five years.

Isaiah is the founder and CEO of Cheeky Scientist, a career training company that specializes in helping PhDs transition into corporate careers; he is also the director of Hankel Leadership. Through these ventures, Isaiah has consulted on career development, employee management, entrepreneurship, focus, and motivation at several Fortune 500 companies. He has been invited to speak at top institutions including Harvard Medical School, Stanford University, Vanderbilt University, the University of Chicago, the University of Oxford, the Marie

Curie Institute France, and the St. Jude Children's Research Hospital.

Isaiah grew up working on a sheep farm in the Pacific Northwest of the U.S. before going on to get his doctorate. After receiving his doctorate, Isaiah started and successfully exited several other technology-based companies, and then went on to be formally trained in the fields of behavioral economics, behavior psychology, and online marketing. Isaiah's blue-collar background, white-collar corporate training, and academic credentials allow him to work with a wide range of organizations and connect meaningfully with all types of individuals and institutions.

INTRODUCTION: WHAT IS INTELLIGENT ACHIEVEMENT?

Try not to become a person of success, but rather try to become a person of value.

—Albert Einstein

Achievement is about value. It's about attaining value through effort and skill.

The question is, what do you currently value?

What are you working to attain?

Have you been taught to value your job title or your relationship with some other person above all else? Have you been convinced that the most valuable things in life are your paycheck, the number of people who say "hello" to you at the office, and the number of people who say "I need you" at home?

Or, have you become so passive in what you value that you let anyone and anything into your life, as long as whatever you let in allows you to stay disconnected from the cold hard truth that when things really go wrong in your life, the only person who will be able to fix it and the only person who will be responsible for it is you.

Welcome to fake success.

Passivity, dependence, and the sacrifice of realism and personal responsibility to whatever fuzzy, grandiose ideal is currently trending in the ether of your mind—these are the markers of fake success.

Fake success is a moving target. It's unstable, as I learned the hard way. I thought staying busy, competing with others at the office, and thinking as big as possible was my meal ticket to permanent achievement. But it was all an illusion. What I had built up in my mind as the pinnacle of existence was dark and empty.

My *laissez-faire* attitude about my attention and where I put it … the mutual feelings of security that came from needing other people and them needing me … the joy and freedom of keeping my head in the clouds so I never had to commit to anyone or anything.

… oh, how I cherished my broken little toys.

Once things went wonky in my life though, I saw just how hollow this kind of fake success is.

Intelligent Achievement, on the other hand, is *not* a moving target. It's *not* empty either. Instead, it's sturdy, full, and immovable.

It's *not* something that's just handed to you. It's *not* something you're nudged into chasing or coerced into wanting.

Intelligent Achievement comes from within you. It's a collection of values that are aligned with who you are—values you have to protect and nurture. These values do not increase your dependence on other people and things. Instead, they relieve you of dependence.

Intelligent Achievement is something that you have a part in building from the ground up—you know what's in it—you chose it, someone else didn't choose it for you. It's instilled with your purpose and it's something you alone are responsible for.

Intelligent Achievement teaches you the scientific process of finding success through your most valuable assets—selective focus, creative ownership, and pragmatic growth—first, by developing your focus and learning how to conserve your mental energy.

If you've failed to reach an important goal because you were distracted, misinformed, or overcommitted, then you know the role focus and selectivity play in achievement.

Second, you will learn how to stop allowing your happiness and success to be dependent on other people. A bank, tax collector, or the government may be able to take away your house, business, savings, stocks, and other indicators of fake success, but they can never take away your knowledge, network, or ability. You must take creative ownership over these three things in your life.

Finally, you will learn the art of changing your life through pragmatic decisions and actions. Self-improvement is not the result of dramatic changes. Instead, personal and professional change is initiated and sustained by consistent, practical changes. To grow, you must leverage the power of micro-decisions, personal responsibility, and mini-habits. Your own biology will not let you improve your life in any other way.

Intelligent Achievement will also show you how to avoid falling into the trap of chasing fake success. What fake success signals have you been pursuing? Your image? Job titles? Annual salary? Facebook friends?

Chasing empty indicators of success has left millions of people in a variety of careers—blue-collar, white-collar, and academics alike—leading a vacuous, shallow life, that leaves them burnt out, dependent, and disconnected.

It's never too late to turn things around. Whether you want to reach higher levels of true achievement in your career or in your personal life, you need to *start valuing the right things now*: selective focus, creative ownership, and pragmatic growth.

Part 1
Selective Focus

*Doing less meaningless work, so that you can focus on things
of greater personal importance is not laziness. This is hard
for most to accept, because our culture tends to reward personal
sacrifice instead of personal productivity.*

—Tim Ferriss

Selectivity is the gateway to productivity. Learning to be highly selective in terms of your attention, and your mental energy levels overall, is the first step on the path towards *Intelligent Achievement*. It is simply impossible to become more successful in life in any way without first protecting your focus.

1 Why Mental Energy is Your Most Valuable Asset

When mental energy is allowed to follow the line of least resistance and to fall into easy channels, it is called weakness.

—James Allen

Nothing can save you from your fatigued mind.

Not time—hours don't matter when your brain is incapable of making good decisions.

Not money—dollars won't buy you clarity or stamina.

Not relationships—how can you make others happy when you can't do it for yourself?

If you've ever sat in front of the TV to watch something you've seen before because you're tired, you know that time is not your most valuable resource. If you've ever bought anything beyond food, water, shelter, or your other basic needs, you know money is not your most valuable resource.

If you've ever wanted to help more people, give more to your current relationships, or build new ones, but were stretched too thin by your current obligations, you know that relationships are not your most valuable resource either.

Mental energy is your most valuable asset. Without it, you won't have the enthusiasm, motivation, drive, and physical energy to live a full life rich in all of those things listed above.

The problem is this asset depreciates rapidly every day. Scientific studies published in the *Harvard Business Review* and by Cambridge University Press point to evidence that you only get about 90–120 minutes of peak mental energy[1] and five hours or less of "near" peak mental energy[2] each day.

For the rest of the day, your mental energy levels are medium to low at best. The good news is that if you get enough sleep, your energy replenishes 100%.

A study published in the journal *Sleep Medicine* reveals that the right amount of REM sleep (four to six cycles) completely restores your mental energy each day.[3] So that's good, but …

Even if you start each day at 100%, your mental energy is going to drop quickly.

That's why you want to cherish your mental energy. Harvest it. Tend to it like a precious garden. And, when necessary, fight for it.

The Fight for Your Mental Energy

Mental energy is the world's hottest commodity. People are going to try to steal it, drain it, and suck it up every second you're awake. Yet very few of us protect it. Few of us know how.

People carefully protect the money in their bank account and the time in their calendar, but they do little to protect their attention. Attention is the gateway to your mental energy. Where your attention goes, your mental energy flows.

And more often than not, it is flowing toward something someone else wants.

Taking back your mental energy is not a cakewalk. It's a *dogfight*.

Even your own mind is going to fight viciously to keep you distracted.

All the "yeses" you've said and all the obligations you've taken on in the past have created a kind of "psychological immune system."

This immune system has evolved to protect your sense of homeostasis. It does so by rejecting any attempts you make to change where you direct your effort. Your brain hates change; it likes distraction. It wants you to stay in this comfort zone of distraction you've created, wasting your energy on the wrong things—so it works to keep you there.

Distraction is safe, see?

There are other rewards, too. Your brain likes the approval you get by saying yes to others. It likes the stimulation of drama and gossip. It likes being a small part of everything and a big part of nothing.

You need to repair this immune system.

Protecting Your Mental Energy

Right now, your psychological immune system is seeking safety. You have trained it, either actively or passively, to fear change.

The only way to reprogram it is to start being more selective with where you spend your mental energy. The first step to protecting your mental energy is to ignore the urge to give your attention to whoever or whatever is seeking your attention.

Build up a resistance against this inclination by saying "no" to everything first. This will be hard to do at first but, over time, it will become easier and easier.

Learn to feel a sense of success when you say "no," rather than a sense of failure.

You've been trained since birth to say "yes" to everything. Every time you agreed to do something your parents or teachers told you to do, you received positive affirmation. Now, you see, saying yes is the key to getting rewarded.

This is a mistake. Saying yes without discretion brings failure, not success. Set "no" as your default response. Start rewarding yourself for being selective. Every time you say "no" you get one step closer to achieving true success.

Most importantly, learn to keep all gossip and meaningless drama out of your life. Nothing will drive your mental energy levels down faster than having an emotional blowout. Defending yourself against gossip at the office is tiring; hard work is not. Fighting with your relationship partner is tiring. Falling out with a friend or family member is tiring. Maintaining healthy relationships is not.

The solution is simple—stop burning through your mental energy on emotional drama. The key to doing this is to learn to walk away from energy draining people.

Energy draining people—think of them as vampires needing the energy of others to survive—grow stronger by feeding on your attention. They play the victim, act out, and create all kinds of drama to steal away your attention. Stop letting these people hijack your focus. Protect your mental energy by walking away from them once and for all.

Saying "no" and removing energy draining people from your life will help rewire your brain so that you're no longer addicted to distraction or drama.

Surround Yourself With Mental Energizers

Once you've learned to protect your mental energy, surround yourself with people and activities that increase your mental energy levels.

There are some people and activities you *should* say yes to, of course. The key is that you need to be selective about who and what you let into your life.

Find people who energize you and keep you on track towards your goals. Then, hold onto them. Find activities that excite you and bring you closer to your goals. Then, keep executing them. These people and activities will ensure that your psychological immune system starts to defend *against* distraction, and *against* drama.

Your mental energy is going to plummet throughout the day, certainly. But that's not a bad thing. It's only bad if it's being wasted on people and activities that are pivoting you away from true success.

Be selective and start saving your most valuable resource—mental energy—for the best things in life, not the worst.

Notes

1. Schwartz, T. and McCarthy, C. (2007) 'Manage your energy, not your time'. *Harvard Business Review*. https://hbr.org/2007/10/manage-your-energy-not-your-time

2. Omahen, D. (2009) 'The 10 000-hour rule and residency training'. *Canadian Medical Association Journal*, 180(1–2): 1272. https://www.ncbi.nlm.nih.gov/pmc/articles/pmc2691450/#b1 –1801272

3. Sasai, T. *et al.* (2012) 'Impaired decision-making in idiopathic REM sleep behavior disorder'. *Sleep Medicine*. 13(3): 301–6. https://www.ncbi.nlm.nih.gov/pubmed/22285107

2 How Busyness Leads to Burnout and Manipulation

Beware the barrenness of a busy life.

—Socrates

Busyness drains mental energy and prevents mastery.

You may have heard that mastering any skill, whether it's business, surgery, playing the violin, or fencing, requires 10,000 hours of practice. What you may not have heard is that this practice is best done in short bursts, not in long drawn-out days.

Scientific studies published in *Psychological Review* have shown over and over again that the fundamental difference between elite versus average performers in any field is the number of hours the elite tier spends on deliberate practice[1]—the uncomfortable, methodical work of stretching your ability to execute a skill.

Elite performers deliberately practice three times longer than average performers.

That's not the surprising part. The surprising part is that the *average performers* practiced more hours overall. So, what gives? The average performers work harder than the elite performers and don't get rewarded for all this effort?

No, they don't. It's how you practice that matters, not how long.

When researchers compared the mean time both sets of performers spent working versus the waking hours of the day, they found that average performers passively spread their work throughout the day.

The elite performers, however, were very selective with their efforts. Instead of spreading their work out passively, they consolidated their work into short bursts. These performers' *working time* versus *waking time* charts showed two sharp peaks—one in the morning and one in the afternoon. Elite performers spent more time in deliberate practice but only worked an average of 3.5 hours a day.

As a result, the elite performers leverage their mental energy more productively. The rest of their time was spent on leisure, relaxation, and recovery.

The Busy Life Versus the Productive Life

There's a right way and a wrong way to live.

Feeling inspired and energized as you execute productive actions that lead to both the achievement of your goals and a sense of fulfillment is the right way to live. Feeling constantly rushed and weighed down by other people's demands and expectations is the wrong way.

No one ever sat on their deathbed wishing they had been busier. No one ever came to the end of their days begging for more time to do things that didn't matter. The only way to live a happy and successful life is to *stop being busy and start being selective.*

Selectivity is the gateway to productivity—and productive people live long, healthy, and fulfilling lives. Busy people who passively fill up their lives with distractions, on the other hand, live short, stressful, and exhausting lives.

Busy people have mental breakdowns, become emotionally burnt-out, and are routinely manipulated by others. The reason busy people suffer so much is that busyness is a gateway to mediocrity, reduced expectations, and reduced willpower.

Busyness leads to giving up on your dreams, following others, and wasting your valuable mental energy levels.

The only way to avoid the busy person's fate is to understand where busyness leads. Once you know the pitfalls busy people face, you can adjust your life to avoid falling into them yourself.

Busy People Become Average

People who brag about being busy will always be average. They will never accomplish anything great or leave a legacy behind them. These people brag about busyness because nothing else in their lives is worth discussing. Being busy does not lead to achievement or fulfillment.

Just the opposite: Busyness prevents the very things it tries to signal.

If you're so busy that you don't have time to breathe, you may be wasting your life; you're certainly wasting your time. You will never get anywhere in life without taking some time for yourself to sit down, look ahead, and see where you're going.

Busy people don't make things happen.

Things just happen to busy people. Life just happens to them. You want to flip that around: to be proactive instead of reactive, to do instead of be done upon. Effectiveness should be your goal, not busyness.

The problem is being busy feels good. The human brain loves feeling busy. You get a dopamine rush every time you cross off an item from your to-do list. It doesn't matter if the item you're crossing off is important or not, you still get a rush. On top of this, telling others that you're busy is an ego boost. Being busy makes you feel important.

Busyness is a drug. And the only way to get off of it is to start obsessing with results.

What's the result of what you're doing? What's the outcome? Is there any value in spending the next eight hours on some side project your coworker wants you to do, or four hours at some event that your family or friends want you to attend? Will either of these things bring you closer to your goals?

If the answer is no, say *no*.

Busy People Are Followers, Not Leaders

You can set your agenda for your life, or you can follow someone else's. The choice is up to you. The biggest problem with being busy all the time is that it keeps you reliant on other people.

Busyness keeps you dependent on the herd. This herd mentality is your brain's default mindset, and it's what you have to actively work against every day if you want to be successful. The only way to stop blindly following others is to stop doing what others want you to do.

That means setting firm boundaries with people and continuing to express your creativity and individuality no matter how much resistance you get. The problem is that others commonly reject creativity and originality. Studies reported in *Psychological Science* show that most people have a negative bias towards creativity.[2]

Most people act like they want you to express yourself openly but, in reality, they don't. Instead, they just want you to stay busy following their agendas.

Busyness is how others control you.

Busyness is how others get you to conform.

Why Busy People are Easily Manipulated

Distracted people get taken advantage of, and busy people are distracted.

When you are busy, it's easy for other people to make you feel like you only have one choice: theirs.

When you're busy, it's easy for other people to make you feel like you need them to be successful.

When you're busy, it's easy for other people to make you feel like it's your duty to take care of them.

Distraction turns people into pushovers.

When grown men and grown women try to make you feel guilty for not spending time with them or not doing what they want, it's simply a power play.

These people know that you have a thousand other things going on and would rather give in to them than feel guilty. They use your busyness against you by making silent threats to play the victim or suck you into drama. As a result, you say yes to everything. You have to say yes. If you don't, you'll have to deal with emotional blackmail.

Staying busy is an easy trap to fall into no matter who you are.

If you want to be average, run around all day in a false sense of busyness. Stay passive and unfocused, only half concentrating on whatever you're doing at the time. Worry constantly. Plan for the worst. Try to fit in, let others boss you around, and say yes to everything. Most importantly, never be selective with your attention.

But, if you want to be productive, if you want to achieve worthwhile goals while feeling a sense of fulfillment, it's time to get focused. You need to start being self-aware enough to reject busy, meaningless activities and, instead, to focus on the one or two things that really matter to you each day.

Notes

1. Ericsson, K. *et al.* (1993) 'The role of deliberate practice in the acquisition of expert performance'. *Psychological Review*, 100(3): 363–406. http://psycnet.apa.org/index.cfm?fa=buy.optionToBuy& id=1993-40718-001

2. Mueller, *et al.* (2010) 'The bias against creativity'. http:// digitalcommons.ilr.cornell.edu/cgi/viewcontent.cgi?article=1457& context=articles

3 The Infection Known as "Other People's Opinions"

It is not advisable to venture unsolicited opinions. You should spare yourself the embarrassing discovery of their exact value to your listener.

—Ayn Rand

A few years ago, I had to get emergency surgery after a negative health diagnosis (see the Preface for the backstory). After the diagnosis, there was no time to think.

My life sped up. Things started happening at warp speed, and I couldn't catch up. I was thrown into a vicious conveyer belt of mandatory action by a team of medical specialists.

After my tests, labs, and surgery, however, things slowed down. Now, there was plenty of time to think—too much time, perhaps. There was also plenty of time to ask for advice.

As often happens during these kinds of traumatic events, I felt a deep sense of loss and confusion. Clearly, I was doing something wrong in life for this to happen ... right? Where did I mess up? What did I need to change? Why was I being punished? I needed answers and I needed answers now.

To find the answers I needed, I asked all my family members and friends for their advice. I went to a variety of therapists, psychiatrists, and counselors. Some of them had very strong opinions on what I was doing wrong and how I should change my life, while others just agreed with whatever I suggested, told me that "it was just bad luck," or kindly admitted that they had no advice to give.

While talking to others was helpful, looking to them to guide me was a mistake. Instead of centering me, everyone's various opinions pulled me apart. Their emotional responses to my emotional situation made me—you guessed it—more emotional. It wasn't until I decided to listen to myself that things started to get better.

Once I took some time for myself—and listened—the answers came. In fact, the answers were always present. There was a small voice inside of me the whole time telling me exactly what I needed to change. The voice told me that I needed to start being more selective. More selective in what I gave my attention to, who I gave my energy to, and certainly, whose advice I listened to.

You Know What's Best For You

Other people's opinions are like viruses. They infect you. No matter who you are or how strong you may be, other people affect your emotions and behavior.

These feelings and actions circulate through social networks in patterns similar to that seen in epidemiological models of the flu virus.

A scientific study published in 2010 in the *Proceedings of the Royal Society* estimated that every positive person you let into your life increases your chances of being positive by 11 percent, but every negative person you let into your life *doubles* your chances of becoming negative.[1]

Yet most people will let just about *anyone* into their lives. Most people are too free with those they let in and what they take in from these people *vis-à-vis* listening to their blather.

They passively let negative people share their limiting beliefs and limiting opinions like, "Your goals are impossible. Only a fool would try to do that." Or, "Your goals are so easy. Anyone can do that."

As counter-intuitive as it seems, most people make better decisions *when they don't ask for other people's opinions.*

Did you get that? Because it's a vital point. You'll do better when you listen to your inner voice, period.

This is because what you want in life is strongly affected by what other people want in life. Just seeing or hearing about what someone else wants, makes you want it too. Other scientific studies reported in the *Journal of Personality and Social Psychology* show that people who watch someone else pursue a goal are more likely to pursue the same one.[2]

In fact, those same studies show that people who simply read about another person pursuing a goal are more prone to seek it, too. Likewise, when you hear advice about what other people want for you, you're more likely to want the same thing. Their advice influences what you want. It can change your motivation, often for the worse.

You Are Biologically Wired to Copy Others

You can't solve a personal problem with someone else's answer. You can't figure out what your limits are by using other people as a yardstick. Most people, when faced with adversity, run to their friends and families to ask for help.

What should I do? They ask them. Or, even worse: *What do I really want? Who am I?* Other people can't answer these questions. You need to find these answers yourself.

The problem is that you've been conditioned to value other people's opinions more than your own. You've been trained to want to be like other people, to think like them. Not only are you taught to listen to other people, you're also biologically wired to copy their behavior.

Mirror neurons in your brain automatically cause you to copy your surroundings.

For decades, scientists have studied the powerful psychological factors that drive you to fit in with your environment and the people in it. These include groupthink,[3] negativity bias,[4] and the chameleon effect.[5] As a result, you are a walking imitation. You are a natural follower.

Our proclivity for going along with the herd can work to our detriment. Scientific research shows that people who are lied to are more likely to lie and cheat.[6] Similar research shows that having an obese friend increases your chances of becoming obese by 171%[7] and having a smoker in your family increases your chances of smoking by 61%.[8] And the influence of others can impact our brain health just as readily.

Negative Opinions Can Rot Your Brain

The first step to having a breakthrough in life is to start ignoring other people's opinions. When it comes to friendly advice, you must learn to be highly selective. This holds particularly true when the advice is negative. Scientific studies reported by *Stanford University News* show that exposure to negativity lasting 30 minutes or more peels away neurons in your hippocampus, the part of your brain responsible for problem-solving.[9]

Yes, negative opinions can literally *rot your brain.*

You might think that allowing negative people to "vent" at you or trying to make them feel better is virtuous. But, in the end, it does not make you a better person. Instead, it reduces your mental energy levels and hurts your performance.

One study examined 120 participants who were asked to talk with or ignore a negative person.[10] After four minutes of interaction, each participant was given a thought exercise that required solid concentration. The participants who ignored the negative people performed better on the thought exercises than those who engaged with the negative people.

Other studies show that always feeling obligated to make other people happy is incredibly destructive. It can lead to burnout,[11] reckless behavior,[12] and even suicide.[13] There is nothing noble about listening to unsolicited opinions, especially unsolicited negative opinions.

Still not convinced? Here's a summary of how negative opinions and negativity can slowly ruin your life:

- 100% chance you will become more negative for each negative person you let into your life.[14] In contrast, each positive person you let into your life increases your chances of becoming positive by only 11%.

- Double your odds of unhappiness.[15] Put another way, one negative friend doubles your chances of becoming unhappy.

- 50% higher risk of dying young.[16] People who give in to worries and demands from negative relationships have a 50% increase in the risk of dying early.

- 34% more likely to have heart problems. Negative relationships boost heart disease risk by 34%.

- Poverty.[17] Negativity is linked to poverty and reduced brain activity.

- Brain damage.[18] Listening to a negative person for just 30 minutes peels away neurons in your hippocampus, the part of your brain that's responsible for problem solving.

- Reduced creativity.[19] People who work for a negative boss are far less creative than those who work for a positive boss.

- Depression and anxiety.[20] Complaining about your problems increases your risk of developing both clinical depression and anxiety.

- Low self-esteem.[21] Listening to or watching negative people interact lowers your self-esteem and makes you more neurotic.

- Poor performance.[22] Engaging with negative people prior to performance tests, rather than ignoring them, decreases test scores.

- Increased pain.[23] Negativity overrides the effect of pain medication in surgery patients.

- Loss of sleep.[24] Negativity enhances the repercussions of poor sleep.

- Early death.[25] People who use negative emotional language have higher rates of mortality.

You know what's best for your life more than other people do. Sure, there's value in learning from others, and you should never be afraid to solicit advice from wise individuals. But there's nothing to be gained from taking in unsolicited opinions, especially when they're negative.

There's a difference between being informed and being weighed down by information. There's also a difference between someone pointing out a problem constructively (with a possible solution in hand), and someone just pointing out the problem. When it comes to your goals and your life, forget other people's opinions.

Instead, be selective. Trust *yourself.* Put your opinions first. Put your interests first. Put your happiness first. Only then will you have the mental energy you need to design a self-regulated and systemized lifestyle that will lead you toward your biggest goals.

Notes

1.   Hill, A. (2010) 'Emotions as infectious diseases in a large social network: the SISa model'. *Proceedings of the Royal Society*. http://rspb.royalsocietypublishing.org/content/277/1701/3827.short

2.   Hassin, R. R. *et al*. (2004) 'Goal contagion: Perceiving is for pursuing'. *Journal of Personality and Social Psychology, 87*(1): 23–37

3.   Rose, J. D. (2011) 'Diverse perspectives on the groupthink theory—A literary review'. *Emerging Leadership Journeys*, 4(1): 37–57. http://www.regent.edu/acad/global/publications/elj/vol4iss1/Rose_V4I1_pp37–57.pdf

4.   Vaish, A. (2013) 'Not all emotions are created equal: The negativity bias in social-emotional development'. *Psychology Bulletin, 134*(3): 383–403. https://www.ncbi.nlm.nih.gov/pmc/articles/PMC3652533/

5.   Chartrand, T. L. and Bargh, J. A. (1999) 'The chameleon effect: the perception-behavior link and social interaction'. *Journal of Personality and Social Psychology, 76*(6): 893–910. https://www.ncbi.nlm.nih.gov/pubmed/10402679

6.   University of California, San Diego (2014) 'Lied-to children more likely to cheat, lie'. *ScienceDaily*. https://www.sciencedaily.com/releases/2014/03/140319093802.htm

7.   Christikis, N. A. and Fowler, J. H. (2007) 'The spread of obesity in a large social network over 32 years'. *New England Journal of Medicine, 357* (4): 370–9. https://www.ncbi.nlm.nih.gov/pubmed/17652652

8.   Rezaeetalab, F. (2012) 'The effect of smoking by family members and friends on the incidence of smoking among high school students'. *Pneumologia*. *61*(4): 234–6. https://www.ncbi.nlm.nih.gov/pubmed/23424948

9.   Schwartz, M. (2007) 'Robert Sapolsky discusses physiological effects of stress'. *Stanford News*. http://news.stanford.edu/news/2007/march7/sapolskysr-030707.html

10.   Sommer, K. and Juran, Y. (2013) 'Ostracism as resource conservation during aversive interactions'. *Journal of Social and Personal*

Relationships. http://journals.sagepub.com/doi/abs/10.1177/
0265407512473006?rss=1&

11. Stechyson, N. (2012) 'Sense of obligation to employer causes
     burnout: study says'. Canada.com. http://www.canada.com/
     Sense+obligation+employer+causes+burnout+study/6410674/
     story.html

12. APA (2014) 'Sense of obligation leads to trusting strangers, study
     says'. http://www.apa.org/news/press/releases/2014/05/trusting-
     strangers.aspx

13. Hastings, M. (2002) 'Shame, guilt, and suicide'. *Suicide Science.*
     pp. 67–79. https://link.springer.com/chapter/10.1007/0–306
     –47233-3_6

14. Hill, A. *et al.* (2010) 'Emotions as infectious diseases in a large
     social network: The SISa model'. *Royal Society Publishing.* http://
     rspb.royalsocietypublishing.org/content/277/1701/3827.short

15. Keim, B. (2014) 'Happiness and sadness spread just like disease'.
     Wired. https://www.wired.com/2010/07/contagious-emotions/

16. Reuters (2014) 'Stressful relationships may lead to early death'. *NY
     Daily News.* http://www.nydailynews.com/life-style/health/stressful-
     relationships-lead-earlier-death-article-1.1806075

17. Doheny, K. (2007) 'Bad marriage, bad heart?: Negative relationships
     boost heart disease risk by 34%, study shows'. WebMD.

18. Zetlin, M. 'Listening to complainers is bad for your brain'. https://
     www.inc.com/minda-zetlin/listening-to-complainers-is-bad-for-
     your-brain.html

19. UNIS (2014) 'In fear of your boss? New UNSW research shows
     you'll be far less creative'. http://www.unisaustralia.com/category/
     business-economics-law-news/

20. APA (2007) 'Someone to complain with isn't necessarily a good
     thing, especially for teenage girls'. http://www.apa.org/news/press/
     releases/2007/07/co-rumination.aspx

21. Ross, R. (2012) 'Study: People who watch reality TV have lower
     self-esteem'. http://www.tvguide.com/news/reality-tv-study-
     1057707/

22. Sommer, K. and Juran, Y. (2013) 'Ostracism as resource conservation during aversive interactions'. *Journal of Social and Personal Relationships.* http://journals.sagepub.com/doi/abs/10.1177/0265407512473006?rss=1&

23. Neergaard, L. (2011) 'Study finds negativity tied to physical pain'. http://www.sj-r.com/x1274021981/Study-finds-negativity-tied-to-physical-pain?Start=1

24. O'Brien, E.M. (2010) 'Negative mood mediates the effect of poor sleep on pain among chronic pain patients'. *Clinical Journal of Pain,* *26*(4): 310–9. https://www.ncbi.nlm.nih.gov/pubmed/20393266

25. Johannes, C. E. *et al.* (2015) 'Psychological language on twitter predicts county-level heart disease mortality'. *Psychological Science.* http://journals.sagepub.com/doi/abs/10.1177/0956797614557867

4 How Small-Minded People Block Big Goals

To be yourself in a world that is constantly trying to make you something else is the greatest accomplishment.

—Ralph Waldo Emerson

As we discussed in the last chapter, your brain sees other people's goals as suggestions for what your goals should be. Whether they're deliberate or not, these suggestions affect your expectations, which impacts your behavior. Put another way, other people can play a determining role in the path your life takes.

A report by *Current Directions in Psychological Science* shows that suggestions create *response expectancies*, or the ways in which we anticipate our responses in various situations.[1]

These expectancies set you up for automatic responses that actively influence how you get to the outcome you expect in any situation. Once you anticipate a particular outcome, your subsequent thoughts and behaviors will help make that outcome happen.

The Power of Suggestion

If a usually timid guy expects a few beers will help him get a girl's phone number, he will feel more confident after he drinks the beers, approach more girls, and get more phone numbers. Though he may give credit to the beers he drank, his expectations of how the beers would make him feel played a big role.

A deliberate suggestion influenced his expectations, which changed his behavior.

However, this guy could have been influenced by non-deliberate suggestions as well. If his friends were watching him, he might act more confidently. If his friend told him that he had a good feeling about tonight, or told him that tonight is a particularly lucky night for him because there's a full moon out, he might believe something lucky would happen and subconsciously act more confidently.

Studies reported in *Psychological Science* confirm that these kinds of non-deliberate suggestions can make people more successful.[2] For example, golfers make more successful putts when they are told that a golf ball is lucky, participants solve motor-dexterity puzzles better when experimenters make a "good luck" hand gesture, and patients perform better on memory games when they're in the presence of their lucky charm.

Your Brain's Herd Mentality

Suggestions from other people are powerful because they tap into your desire to fit in. This desire is driven by several biological processes, most notably your brain's herd mentality. Studies published in *Science* magazine on herd mentality, or groupthink (or "swarm intelligence") show that humans, animals, and even insects, respond to external changes with very low levels of cognition.[3]

Large groups are often led, not by the conscious choices of each individual, but by a mob-like collection of dull, subconscious responses. The best example of this behavior is shown in the Solomon Asch experiment.[4]

The Asch experiment was first conducted in 1951 when Asch, a psychologist, brought together small groups of college students for a "visual perception study." But instead of testing visual perception, the study was testing the effects of herd mentality.

During the experiment, every student, except one, was a planted actor who knew the nature of the research. The players were instructed to give *incorrect* answers to basic questions that involved matching black lines on white cards.

The real subject, who was the only one not aware of the actual experiment, was asked each question after hearing the planted actors' answers. Again and again (up to 36% of the time), the subject knowingly answered incorrectly against clear visual evidence in order to fit in with the group.

This is the equivalent of saying the sky is green just because four other people said it first.

The Liberating Power of Defiance

Subtle suggestions from other people affect your behavior. They can positively change your behavior. But, if you're not careful, the power of suggestion can also negatively change your behavior. That holds true for your future actions, too. If you're not selective with who you surround yourself with, your life can easily and negatively be affected by the power of suggestion. If you're not selective, there will be a heavy influence on you to pursue small goals, settle for mediocrity, and sustain the status quo.

The only way to achieve what you want in life—your biggest and truest goals—is to defy your herd mentality.

Going against the grain will not only liberate you from negative mental loops (which we'll discuss in depth later), it will liberate others as well. Indeed, when another actor was planted in Asch's experimental group and instructed to provide a truthful answer in the face of a misleading majority, the error rate dropped from 36% to 5.5%.[5] In other words, all it took was one person to disagree with the majority to free someone else from their desire to fit in. This is the liberating power of defiance. This is the power you can tap into at will when you choose to be selective instead of passive with your attention.

Notes

1. Michael, R. B. *et al.* (2012) 'Suggestion, cognition, and behavior'. http://journals.sagepub.com/doi/abs/10.1177/0963721412446369
2. Ibid.

3. Couzin, D. *et al.* (2013) 'Emergent sensing of complex environments by mobile animal groups'. *Science 339*(6119): 574–576.
   http://science.sciencemag.org/content/339/6119/574

4. The Asch Experiment. YouTube. https://www.youtube.com/watch?
   v=qA-gbpt7Ts8

5. Asch, S. (1955) 'Opinions and social pressures'. *Scientific American.*
   http://www.lucs.lu.se/wp-content/uploads/2015/02/Asch-1955-
   Opinions-and-Social-Pressure.pdf

5 Scientific Proof That 50% of Your Friendships are Fake

Associate yourself with people of good quality, for it is better to be alone than in bad company.

—Booker T. Washington

Some people don't want you to be successful. Even some of your so-called friends or colleagues don't want you to get ahead. They might say they do, but behind their big toothy grins and pats on the back, they want to see you held back—or at least behind or below them.

Scientific researchers from the University of Tel Aviv and MIT found that, in general, everyone is pretty terrible at accurately perceiving our friendships.[1] Our judgment is so bad that for every one real friend we have, we also have one fake friend. The study concluded the following:

"We found that 95 percent of participants thought that their relationships were reciprocal," Dr. Shmueli says. "If you think someone is your friend, you expect him to feel the same way. But in fact that's not the case—only 50 percent of those polled matched up in the bidirectional friendship category."

In other words, only 50% of your friendships are reciprocal. The rest of your friendships are one-sided or fake. Online friendship groups fare even worse on the scale of true or false, says another scientific study published by the Royal Society.[2]

In measuring friendships, the MIT researcher's algorithm found that lack of reciprocity or a "unidirectional" relationship occurred in many of the friendships that we could identify as being our closest and best.

What does this mean? It means that even some of your "best" friends are fake. Think about that. Are you surprised? I bet you're not. I bet deep down you knew for a long time that some of your so-called friends were not really who you made them out to be.

There's nothing better than a true friendship—a reciprocal friendship. People in reciprocal relationships enjoy greater progress and overall success as a result of that influence. These true friendships are precious.

The director of the Gallup Organization, Tom Rath, published his bestseller, *Vital Friends*, which discussed research showing that true friendships can improve your life in a variety of ways. For example, if you have healthy friends, you are five times more likely to be healthy yourself. If you have a good friend at work, you are seven times more likely to be engaged in your job.[3]

Having genuine friendships that are positive makes you better at what you do. They make life more enjoyable and meaningful. But just as a real friend can improve your life in every way, a fake friend can destroy your life in every way. So the question becomes, how can you best distinguish a true friend from a fake friend? How can you ensure that you are selecting the former and disassociating with the latter?

Why Fake Friendships are Irrational

Life is much simpler than most people want you to believe. You do x, and you get y. That's it. It's a simple math equation. The problem is the average person thinks he deserves y just because he wants it. This person has been taught to believe that he can achieve y just by talking about it, just by being a good person, or just by being born. This is nonsense.

According to the book *Discrete Mathematics with Applications*, if x is a necessary cause of y, then the presence of y necessarily implies the presence of x.[4] In other words, you can't deserve y when you haven't done x. You certainly can't achieve y without doing x.

You cannot deserve something you have not earned, including friendship. When you believe you deserve something you have not earned, you're evading reality. You're trying to reverse the law of causality. You're trying to have your cake and eat it too.

Fake friends want unearned respect, as if respect—the effect—could give them personal value—the cause. They want unearned admiration, as if admiration—the effect—could give them virtue—the cause. Sometimes they want unearned money too, as if money—the effect—could give them ability—the cause. They turn to you to give them these things.

Once you know the warning signs of fake friendships and understand the logical fallacy of staying in a fake friendship, you can walk away guilt-free and start living your life with a lot more mental energy.

Signs You Are Stuck in a Fake Friendship

The first sign you are caught in a one-sided friendship is when someone tries to use the fact that they care about you as leverage to control your behavior.

You can care about anyone you want. You don't need permission to care. Likewise, other people can care about you whether or not you say so. However, just because someone chooses to care about you it does not mean you must care about them the same way in return.

Sure, it's healthy to be polite and cordial to people in general. But do not confuse politeness with penance. You don't owe other people anything.

Just because someone likes you does not mean you have to like them. Just because someone considers you in their decisions does not mean you have to consider them. It sounds harsh, but it's true.

You must guard yourself against feeling like you owe other people things just because they care about you. Otherwise, these people will take advantage of you by playing the victim.

The second sign is when someone expects you to take their feelings into account for every decision you make about your own life. Your happiness is independent of anyone else's happiness. No one has a right to tie their happiness to you and your actions without your permission, and then expect you to behave in a way that keeps them happy.

No one has any claim to your time just because you spent time with them in the past. Likewise, no one has any claim to your feelings just because you had feelings for them in the past.

Sure, if you have kids or commit to a long-term work or personal relationship, you've bonded your happiness with the happiness of others. But this only goes so far.

At the end of the day, everyone is responsible for their own happiness. You're not responsible for how someone else feels. You can't *feel* for anyone else. A person's feelings are the effect of that person's decisions alone. You're not responsible for causing other people's happiness.

Happiness is a personal decision and it's up to each of us to decide to be happy.

The third sign you are stuck in a fake friendship is when someone asks you for a handout and expects you to pretend that they earned it.

There are too many people asking for charity today. Crowdfunding platforms like GoFundMe, Kickstarter, and IndieGoGo have been great tools for helping entrepreneurs get their businesses off of the ground and helping people support each other when there's real need.

However, these tools have also been used destructively. They have been used by people who have nothing to offer in return and who are not really in need—individuals who simply want other people to give them money, energy, and attention for doing nothing.

The biggest problem with crowdsourcing platforms is they encourage people to ask for charity while simultaneously asking you, the funder, to pretend that it's not. These campaigns work to convince you that you're investing in other people when you're just giving your money away.

On a more practical level, we all have a friend who has invited us over to their house to listen to some multi-level marketing scheme.

Don't miss this opportunity to invest in a timeshare property.

Or,

Invest in your health by buying this essential oil, supplement, or special formulation of XYZ.

What these fake friends are really asking you to do is to give them money, not because they earned it, but simply because you've spent time with them.

No one deserves other people's time, money, or resources. These things must be earned.

Fake friends and negative people are going to come into your life. It's up to you either to passively accept them and deal with the consequences, or to be selective with who you give your attention to and take steps to distance yourself as soon as possible. Being selective with your friendships will help ensure that you are filling your life with reciprocal relationships. Of course, it's up to you to reciprocate and hold up your end of the equation by being a true friend in return.

Notes

1. American Friends of Tel Aviv. (2016) 'We are bad judges of friendship, new study shows'. https://www.sciencedaily.com/releases/2016/05/160505140917.htm

2. Dunbar, R. I.M. (2016) 'Do online social media cut through the constraints that limit the size of offline social networks?' http://rsos.royalsocietypublishing.org/content/3/1/150292

3. Collingwood, J. (2016) 'The Importance of Friendship'. *Psych Central.* Retrieved on September 18, 2017, from https://psychcentral.com/lib/the-importance-of-friendship/

4. Epp, S. *Discrete Mathematics with Applications.* http://fit.ac.ir/en/download/ebooksclub.org__Discrete_Mathematics_with_Applications.pdf

6 How to Deal With Negative People Without Becoming Negative

You can either be a victim of the world or an adventurer in search of treasure. It all depends on how you view your life.

—Paulo Coelho

The people you allow in your life will affect your emotions, your decisions, and your actions.

Most importantly, they will affect your *options*.

You'll never reach your full potential if you keep giving your valuable time and energy to negative people. Stop letting everyone into your life. Start making room for your biggest dreams. Create space for new, positive people who will support you and like you just the way you are.

If you've already let negative people into your life, cut them out. If you can't cut them out, use them to your advantage. The key is to deal with these negative people without becoming a negative person yourself.

Your adversary is your advisor. Very often, you can leverage other people's negative energy to your advantage, transforming it into positive and productive energy.

A few years ago, I heard a story about the Atlantic codfish. These fish were in high demand in America at the turn of the century, as news of how good these fish taste spread across the country all the way to the West Coast. But there was a problem. How could the West Coast restaurants that wanted to serve Atlantic codfish get the fish across the country and still keep them fresh?

They tried to freeze the fish and send them by rail, which was the fastest means at the time. But, when the West Coast restaurants received the fish and prepared them, they turned out to be very mushy and lacked flavor.

A little later, someone decided to try shipping the fish live by turning the railroad cars into huge saltwater aquariums. When the Atlantic codfish arrived at the West Coast restaurants, they were still alive. But, when they were prepared, they were still mushy and tasteless.

A few years down the road, a young scientist started studying the codfish and discovered that their natural enemy was the catfish. The scientist recommended that the West Coast restaurants ship the codfish in the huge saltwater aquariums as before but this time with a few catfish.

The catfish chased the codfish all the way across the country to the West Coast restaurants. When the codfish arrived and were prepared, they were flaky and had the same flavor as when they were caught fresh. The catfish kept the codfish from becoming stale. In the same way, if you have a negative person in your life that you can't escape by traditional means—walking away, ignoring them, going around them—then use them to your advantage. Learn from them. Turn them into your advisor.

Channel their negative energy into positive action. Let these people sharpen you until you're in a position to leave them behind forever.

The Fog Technique Versus the Investment Technique

Without a defined target to attack, negative people can't hurt you. So, the best way to deal with them is to conceal your goals. By doing this, you prevent them from working against you in the future.

You take away their targets.

If they don't know what you really want, they can't hold you back from it.

I learned the value of this through personal experience.

In my last year of graduate school, I made the mistake of telling my advisor that I wanted to get a non-academic job after getting my PhD. A few months later when we got into a dispute, he used this information against me. He purposely held me back to keep me from taking a position at a company that wanted to hire me just because the company was outside of academia.

After I had missed out on this first job, I decided to stop talking to my advisor about my future career plans. I let it seem as though I wasn't in a hurry to graduate and that I would probably just take some time off and travel. Without a defined target to attack—without a goal to work against—my advisor was left disarmed. In the same way, you can neutralize the negative people in your life by creating a fog around your goals. Resist showing negative people your cards because they might play them against you.

Some negative people have little value, *others are highly valuable*. In fact, it's very likely that someone who you consider to be negative in your life right now is smarter or more talented than you. Why fight them? Why not honor them? By honoring them, you can recruit them to your cause.

The negative people we encounter in life often have similar interests to us, which is why we come across them in the first place. Don't let your own emotions cloud the fact that some negative people have qualities that could benefit you. For example, if a negative person is effectively damaging your reputation online, you could hire them for their online promotional skills. Likewise, if a negative person is stealing your biggest clients, you could buy them out or strike up a partnership.

The best way to disarm negative people is to honor them. By accepting a negative person, you can earn a level of trust and respect from them that surpasses even the confidence and respect of a close friend.

You see examples of this disarmament in business all the time, whereby a top salesperson or other employee at one company is "poached", or offered an elevated position by a competing company. The competing company doesn't attack the other company's employee or try to derail his career, instead, the company honors him.

If someone in your life is annoying, step back and evaluate the situation. See if there's anything about that person worth your investment. Once invested, you two can work together against mutual competitors instead.

Negativity Versus the Void

You can also remove yourself altogether. Individuals, companies, and even countries have used this "void technique" for hundreds of years.

For example, in 1812, Napoleon invaded Russia. Instead of engaging Napoleon in battle, the Russians offered no resistance. They just retreated further and further into their country. As Napoleon and his men marched deeper into Russia without being engaged, they became increasingly agitated, desperate, and weak. Without battle, Napoleon's army had no victory, no direction, no morale boost, and no food or supplies to plunder; they grew as stale as a westbound codfish.

Napoleon made one rash decision after another, pushing his weakened army further east in an attempt to elicit a response from the Russians. By the time he reached Moscow, his initial force of 450,000 men had been reduced to 100,000 by disease and starvation. Napoleon was defeated, not by the Russians, but by the void the Russians created.

Negative people need you to survive. They need you to channel their frustrations and failures because bringing you down makes them feel better. But, when you disappear—when you create a "void"—you force negative people to carry the full weight of their troubles themselves.

The void technique will draw negative people closer to you before removing them altogether. Once negative people realize you're no longer interacting with them, they will do everything within their power to get you to re-engage. Since they've been close to you in the past, they'll know exactly how to bait you into conflict.

Fight the urge to engage. It will get worse, but then it will get better—much better. The key is to *trust the void*. The void is the pinnacle of selectivity. By walking away, avoiding someone or something completely, or quitting a bad habit or bad person by going cold turkey, you leverage the void and protect your most valuable resource—your mental energy.

Case Study #1: Rome Scriva

It was a near death experience, in my opinion.

Rome Scriva's body started shutting down.

She could no longer walk and had to be carried to the emergency room. Her body was burnt from the inside out. Her skin was falling off; her face was bloody. Her two young boys didn't recognize her anymore, and her husband was preparing himself to be left alone to raise them.

After dozens of doctor's appointments, a laundry list of medications, and many nights in the hospital, the doctor's best guess was that she was overworked. Rome had recently left a full-time job to start her own health clinic. Her first clinic became more successful than she imagined, so she opened another.

Soon, Rome had three to manage, and it was taking its toll. But Rome was up to the task. What she was not able to handle was building her business while saying "yes" to everyone and everything else in her life.

Most people stop taking on other obligations when they start a business, especially one in the health industry, but not Rome. She kept trying to be there for everyone in her life. Worse, she kept listening to all of them.

Rome's circle of "friends" had become toxic. Many of the people she was working with had become toxic too. The hard work wasn't killing her. The toxicity of her friends, colleagues, partners, and their opinions—not to mention the stress of managing it all—was killing her. In retrospect, these people had always been toxic; Rome just hadn't noticed it before. Their toxicity had built up over time.

After months and months of doctor's visits, Rome finally started saying "no" to others AND to herself. Being in a position of authority in her business required a lot of self-sacrifice—sometimes, too much.

Enough was enough. Rather than push harder to try to make the third clinic successful (from a hospital bed no less), Rome decided to let it go.

She packed up shop and labeled it a "failure." A much-needed failure. Recovery was slow for Rome. She had ten blood transfusions and sixteen ice therapy baths. Her hair fell out, and her chest became permanently numb. But then she started to get better.

Rome started saying "no" even more. She stopped answering emails in the morning. She stopped picking up her phone first thing too. The people who mattered in her life stepped forward, and those who didn't faded into the background. Rome got better still. When people asked her how she was feeling, she always said "fantastic" even if she felt terrible. She reinforced health and vitality into her mind and body every day—and her mind and body listened.

Walking out of the hospital door with her head held high, Rome said the biggest lesson she learned from the experience was to be assertive and always keep your poise. You don't have to accept other people's opinions or expectations for your life. You can draw a line in the sand and do it with a smile on your face.

Rome carried this lesson over into every area of her life and now is happy, clear, healed, and her two boys recognize her again.

7 Why You Need to Go on a Relationship Fast

You must take personal responsibility. You cannot change the circumstances, the seasons, or the wind, but you can change yourself. That is something you have charge of.

—Jim Rohn

One of the first things I did after recovering from my diagnosis and surgery was go on a relationship fast (see the Preface for the backstory).

I did not cut everyone out of my life during this time—that would have been foolish, especially during such a difficult time. Instead, I removed all of the negative and manipulative people who had been distracting me and filling my life with drama. In short, I removed all the people who I knew were not good for me and who were not aligned with the changes I wanted to make to my life.

I also removed the people who *I* was not good for. This latter part was very difficult.

I knew there were some people in my life who had certain goals that I was not aligned with. There were also people who I had never made a priority even though they had made me a priority.

Instead of keeping these people around merely as an option to call upon selfishly when I needed, or merely as an outlet when I felt like being distracted and felt like being distracting, I let them go. I let them go for their sake, not just mine.

These goodbyes were excruciatingly hard at first, compounding my sense of loss after the trauma I had just been through. Slowly, however, things got easier.

By choosing to be very selective with who I allowed in my life, my life opened up in front of me. Suddenly, I felt surrounded with more space, and gifted with more time. A pleasant void had been created. Before long, new, positive, loyal, and aligned people started filling this void.

You Have to Say Goodbye First

Positive and negative people are like oil and water—they don't mix, ever. Removing the influence of negative people from your life will create space for the supportive, uplifting influence of positive people.

That's the first step: remove the wrong people from your life.

The second step is to spend some time alone working on yourself. What do you want? Who are you, really? The only way to find the right answers to these questions is to spend some time alone. In other words, *you need to go on a relationship fast.*

A relationship fast should last at least a week and no more than a year. During this time, you should remove your obligations to other people and spend time alone, figuring out what you want and who you are.

Of course, be sure to communicate your fast to others in your life. You don't have to tell them exactly what you're doing, but you should say that you'll be unavailable to them for a certain amount of time because you need to work on an important project. (You don't need to mention that you are the project.)

There may be some people, such as your spouse and children, with whom you'll merely have to limit your time. That's okay! The key is to set up firm boundaries so that you can get the most out of your fast. Most importantly, don't feel guilty for this fast. You can't take care of others until you take care of yourself.

What You Will Learn During a Relationship Fast

The first thing you'll learn when you go on a relationship fast is a stronger sense of your individuality, desires, and goals. Most people never achieve this level of clarity. Instead of being an individual, these people have become a combination of the half dozen people they hang out with the most. If you're the kind of person who always needs to be around others, becoming a combination of others instead of a unique individual is unavoidable.

The more time you spend with others, the more like them you will become.

Remember, this is biological. You can't override the mirror neurons in your brain driving you to copy the motivations and behaviors of other people. The only way to truly figure out who you are is to spend some time alone with yourself. And to do it productively.

When you do get time alone, start asking the tough questions that most people avoid. What are your real priorities in life? If money were no object, how would you spend your time? What do you want to achieve before you die? What makes you genuinely happy? Until you know the answers to these questions, you're not an individual. Instead, you're just a composite of other people's hopes and dreams.

The second thing you'll learn is how much you can withstand. *You are stronger than you realize.* You are more mentally tough than you know. Or, maybe you're not. Maybe you're weak and will crumble like a crumb cake when the going gets tough.

Either way, the only way to find out the limits of what you can take and what you can dish out is to stop relying on other people for advice and comfort. Learn to be selective. Learn to heed your own counsel. Learn to comfort yourself.

Put yourself in a challenging situation, one where you either have to win on your own or go down fighting. Step away from the cozy herd and put yourself in unfamiliar territory. Create a time-sensitive goal that you must achieve quickly or fail at embarrassingly. Until you do this, you'll never really know how much you're capable of doing.

Why Your Entire Life is *Your* Fault

The third and final thing you will learn is how to rely on yourself. You are responsible for your problems. Your parents are not to blame. Your negative friends are not at fault. You are responsible. Your entire life is *your fault*.

The problem is that you've let society convince you that your problems are other people's problems. You've fallen into the trap of thinking that everyone shares problems. The human race is not some giant garbage disposal ready to catch your garbage. You need to dispose of it yourself.

As harsh as it sounds, everything bad that's ever happened to you is your responsibility. Bad things happen for no reason. Bad people do bad things. These things are not your fault. *But how you handle them is on you.*

Life is not what happens to you; it's how you handle what happens to you. Don't agree with me? It doesn't matter. Life will decide. Sooner or later, you'll be faced with a situation where no one can help you but yourself. Going on a relationship fast—and doing the work that comes with it—is the fast track to clarity and meaningful change.

The good news is that once you go on a relationship fast and take responsibility for everything in your life, your brain will help you get through any challenges you are currently facing. Scientific studies show that personal responsibility arouses cognitive dissonance,[1] the state of having inconsistent thoughts, beliefs, or attitudes—especially as relating to behavioral decisions and attitude changes. Personal responsibility will help you confront your cognitive dissonance, which can work to your benefit by motivating you to address any misalignment.

By taking responsibility for your past, you are more likely to boost your mood and outlook, too. Why? Because now you have skin in the game—now you are responsible. As a result, your brain will work to make you feel better about your past and create a positive future. This in turn will relieve mental strain and help restore your mental energy levels. The key is that it's your choice to take responsibility. No one can do it for you.

Note

1. Cooper, J. (1971) 'Personal responsibility and dissonance: The role of foreseen consequences'. *Journal of Personality and Social Psychology, 18*(3): 354–363. http://psycnet.apa.org/journals/psp/18/3/354/

8 Automaticity, Scaling, and the Rise of Mental Loops

If you can't describe what you're doing as a process, you don't know what you're doing.

—W. Edwards Demming

Success relies on scalability, which relies on systems, or loops.

Successful people are normal people who have learned how to scale themselves really well. If you don't know what the word "scale" means in the last sentence, don't worry; you are not alone. Most people don't know what it means, or they pretend to know as they smile and nod at their boss.

Here, the word "scale" refers to scalability, which is a characteristic of a system, model or function that describes the system's capability to cope and perform under an increased or expanding workload.

A system that scales well, then, will be able to maintain or even increase its level of performance or efficiency when tested by larger operational demands.

In life, if you know how to scale, you know how to get more and more done without burning out or being miserable. Scaling is what will allow you to free up your time *while* increasing your productivity.

Systemization is what makes scaling possible.

You can't scale without a system.

Recall from above that scalability, by definition, is a characteristic of a system. A system can be simple, like the one you use to brush your teeth the same way every morning, or they can be complex, like the system a business uses to ensure that the contents of every tube of toothpaste they produce are perfect every time.

In today's world, these systems are referred to as loops. Whether you're seeking success in business or life, your scalability will determine your success. Your scalability will be decided by the quality of your internal and external systems or loops.

As technology continues to take over everything from social interactions to the world's economy, the only loops that are worth influencing are those within your own brain (mental loops). If you accept this (and assuming you want to be more successful in life), the question you should be asking yourself right now is, "How can I successfully influence my mental loops?"

Self-Regulation Versus Automaticity

Success relies on scaling and scaling relies on systems. Systemization or, for our purposes, the process of creating a mental loop, relies on both self-regulation and a scientific concept known as "automaticity".

Self-regulation is when a person governs themself without outside assistance or influence.[1] An example of self-regulation is when you limit, of your own accord, how much you will eat.

Willpower, which we'll discuss in detail in Part 3 of this book, is a tool your brain commonly uses to regulate your actions. Going back to our previous example, you may use your willpower to limit how much you will eat. The problem is that willpower needs recharging every 24 hours, making it a weak self-regulation tool.

Numerous studies have shown that using willpower relies on making choices and making choices impairs subsequent self-regulation.[2] Now, we have two problems. The first is that willpower is a limiting resource. The second is that willpower depletes mental energy as it's used, which leads to making bad decisions.

Poor decision-making leads to a further reduction in willpower, which can lead to even worse decisions.

On and on this goes ... until it's Friday night after the end of a long week at the office and you're either six drinks deep at the bar with your friends or home on the couch with a pint of ice cream and Netflix.

Returning one last time to our original self-regulation example, you could also use a habit to limit how much you will eat.

Habits, which we'll also discuss in Part 3 of this book, do not require decision-making. As such, they allow for self-regulation without the energy-depleting effect of willpower. Simple, right?

Not so fast.

Habits are the most commonly misunderstood tools of self-regulation. Most people believe that habits are simply actions that someone carries out consistently. If you tie your shoes every day, then you have a habit of tying your shoes. If you brush your teeth every day, then you have a habit of brushing your teeth. As a result, the concept of creating a good habit is reduced down to the number of times you take a particular action.

However, in reality, habits have very little to do with frequency,[3] and everything to do with "automaticity."

How Mental Loops Will Improve Your Life

Automaticity is at the heart of every mental loop. Automaticity is the ability to do things without occupying the mind with the low-level details required, allowing it to become an automatic response pattern, system, or habit.[4] It is usually the result of learning, repetition, and practice. In other words, automaticity is what makes any automatic system possible. The more automaticity you actively design into your daily lifestyle, the more successful you will be over the course of your life.

Everything in your life can be automated. In fact, over 100 years of experimental psychology research has revealed that social interaction, evaluation and judgment, and the operation of internal goal structures, can all proceed *without* the intervention of conscious acts of will and guidance of the process.[5]

Do you realize the magnitude of the last statement?

All your relationships, every decision you make in life, and all of your wants and needs can be achieved and maintained unconsciously. Now, this is not something I personally want in my life and I doubt you want to go through your life like a zombie either, but that's not the point. The point is you can turn any part of your life on autopilot at any time; which, as it turns out, is the only way to free up the mental energy necessary to further improve your life.

There are many reasons why most people fail to harness this power of automaticity in life. The immense level of clutter that the majority of us have allowed into our lives is the leading culprit.

Another is the high degree of dependency most people have on a single source of income, such as being dependent on one job or one boss for success. In business, this dependency could come from a single source of revenue, such as one flagship product or one big client.

The third reason why people fail to tap into the power of automaticity is that their life is too routine.

That's right—*routine and automaticity are not the same things*. Routine is an activity that is performed as part of a regular procedure rather than for a special reason. Automaticity is when an activity is performed automatically for a special reason. In other words, automaticity requires purpose.

Passivity of focus is the common thread that binds together the three reasons why people fail to harness the power of automaticity. Whether you are distracted by the clutter of negative people or meaningless activities in your life, distracted by the financial instability of a mortgage, school loan, or low paying job, or distracted by the lack of adventure and inventiveness in your life, your mental energy levels, and productivity levels will suffer.

Being selective with your focus is the key to achieving automaticity. The next chapter will start the conversation about how you can stop being distracted and start building a life that automatically brings you the type and level of success you want for yourself.

Notes

1. Carver, C. S. and Scheier, M. F. (1981) *Attention and Self-regulation: A Control-Theory Approach to Human Behavior*. Springer-Verlag, New York (doi: 10.1007/978–1–4612–5887–2).

2. Vohs, K. *et al.* (2014) 'Making choices impairs subsequent self-control: A limited-resource account of decision making, self-regulation, and active initiative'. *Motivation Science*, 1(S): 19–42 http://psycnet.apa.org/journals/mot/1/S/19/

3. Gardner, B. (2012) 'Habit as automaticity, not frequency'. *European Health Psychologist*, 14(2): 32–36. https://www.researchgate.net/publication/230576965_Habit_as_automaticity_not_frequency

4. Bargh, J. A. (1997) 'The automaticity of everyday life'. In R. J. Wyer (ed.), *The automaticity of everyday life: Advances in social cognition* (Vol. 10, pp. 1–61). http://acmelab.yale.edu/sites/default/files/1997_the_automaticity_of_everyday_life.pdf

5. Bargh, A. and Ferguson, M. J. (2000) 'Beyond behaviorism: on the automaticity of higher mental processes'. *Psychology Bulletin*, 126(6): 925–45. https://www.ncbi.nlm.nih.gov/pubmed/11107883

9 Tracking Emotions and Predicting Feelings

Humans: such a brilliant model of emotional self-awareness.

—Charles Stross

Focus is the biggest differentiator between massively successful people and those who just eke their way through life. As mentioned in previous chapters, protecting your mental energy through selectivity is exceptionally hard in today's world. This is because everyone and everything in your life is vying for your attention.

This includes large companies, television commercials, pop-up ads, fake friends, true friends, beggars on the street, and even me right now (thank you for reading). Studies on "decision fatigue" (discussed in Part 3 of this book) show that every unit of attention that you give away to one of these factors decreases your mental energy levels and can lower the level of control you have over your emotions.

Contrary to popular belief, eliminating distractions is *not* the first step to protecting your mental energy and emotions. As you will see time and time again in this book, mental loops require triggers.

In this case, the first step to protecting your mental energy and emotions is not eliminating distractions; it's tracking your attention.

Tracking your attention will lead to activating elimination loops in your brain. First, you must track your mental energy levels, or when your attention is sharp versus when it is dull and distracted.

Second, you must track your emotions, or when you are happiest, on average, throughout the day, as well as when you are the most frustrated and the most depressed. Tracking and measuring your energy levels and emotional states is the only way to manage them and organize your day around them.

When are Your Energy Levels and Emotions Peaking?

Starting when you wake up in the morning, on your phone or a little piece of paper in your pocket, write down every hour of the day that you're awake: 7 a.m., 8 a.m., 9 a.m., 10 a.m. and so on all the way to your bedtime. Then, right next to these hourly times, rate your mental energy levels on a scale of 1 to 10, with 1 being very low mental energy levels and 10 being very high. Do this for three days and look at the trends.

When are your mental energy levels peaking? These are the hours you need to start protecting, the time you should be using to advance your most important personal and professional goals. Conversely, when do your mental energy levels start to crash? These are the hours when you should plan activities like eating or exercise to boost your mental energy levels back up, or when you should plan to do lower energy tasks like answering emails.

Remember, you only get about 90–120 minutes of peak mental energy levels and five hours (or less) of near peak mental energy levels each day. Completing this tracking exercise over the course of at least three days is the only way to identify when these peak states are for you.

After tracking your mental energy levels, you can apply the same strategy to track your emotional states. For example, you can monitor your frustration levels throughout the day by asking yourself every hour: "How angry and defiant am I feeling right now?" Use this time to power through a difficult task on your own, not to do a conference call with a bunch of people who annoy you.

Next, track your happiness levels. When do you feel the most joy during the day? When do you feel the most peace? Schedule activities during these times that will extend this emotional state for you. Go on a nature walk during these times. Play with your kids during these times. Hang out with your friends during these times.

You can make this awareness a practice for as many emotions as you choose. The key is to focus on tracking one emotional state at a time (for at least three days) before moving on to tracking another.

Emotional Predictions Protect Against Emotional Decisions

By tracking our energy and emotions, you can leverage them to your advantage. You can organize your day so that everything you do aligns with your mental energy levels and emotional states. Most importantly, you can use this information to predict how you are going to feel and when you are going to feel this way.

Most people make the mistake of believing they have no control over their emotions. They believe that they have very little control over how they feel. When these people get in a mood, they stay there. As a result, they make emotional decisions, often having to spend large amounts of time and energy correcting these decisions later.

Other people make the mistake of believing that they can easily change their emotional state just by deciding to change it. The truth is your emotions are very powerful and can control you no matter how desperately you "want" to be in control or want to *choose* to be happy. Being selective with your emotions may be hard, especially when you've reached your willpower limit for the day, but predicting your emotions is very easy once you've collected enough data.

Mastering your emotions means knowing which emotions you will experience and when you will experience them. Emotions are not magic. Instead, they are simply a product of your focus and your physiology.

If you're focused on everything that is going wrong in your life, you will likely experience negative emotions. If you focus on everything that is great in your life, you will likely experience positive emotions.

Similarly, if you fail to get a good night's sleep and skip breakfast, you will likely experience negative emotions in the morning, but if you sleep well and eat a healthy breakfast, you will likely experience positive emotions in the morning. By tracking and measuring your emotions over the course of at least three days, you put yourself in a position to identify your patterns.

Once you've identified these trends, you can start predicting how you will feel at certain times of the day. You also put yourself in the position to select the right activities for each emotional state, which in turn will protect your mental energy levels and improve your productivity.

10 How to Label and Close Your Brain's Open Loops

There comes a time when you have to choose between turning the page and closing the book.

—Josh Jameson

The Zeigarnik Effect describes your brain's tendency to finish what it starts. You started unpacking after a trip but had to stop halfway through, and now it's all you can think about (or you waited to start unpacking because you knew you didn't have time to finish completely).

You started listening to a catchy song in the car on the way to work but park before the song finishes, and now the song is stuck in your head. These are examples of the Zeigarnik Effect.

If something you've started doesn't get completed, you will experience *cognitive dissonance*, which is the state of having inconsistent thoughts, beliefs, or attitudes, especially as relating to behavioral decisions and attitude change. You will experience this dissonance even as your conscious mind focuses and executes new tasks and goals. However, this dissonance will distract you, deplete your mental energy, and reduce your performance, sometimes subtly and sometimes not so subtly.

How the Zeigarnik Effect Affects Your Energy and Emotions

In her doctoral thesis, Zeigarnik spent time studying this effect firsthand. She specifically notes the fact that waiters in restaurants are able to remember complex orders long enough to deliver them to the table.[1]

However, once the food is delivered, the order information is forgotten altogether. Instead, the waiters begin to focus on the uncompleted orders from other tables until they, too, are fulfilled and forgotten.

It's nearly 100 years since Zeigarnik published her work and, since then, many other studies[2] have shown that you remember the things you don't complete more than you remember the things you do.

For example, when participants are asked to finish a puzzle but are interrupted in the middle of their work, they remember the details of their suspended task 90% better than for tasks they completed without interruption. But do they remember the details of the interrupted task better? And what happens if the interrupted task never gets done?

Refusing to finish or eliminate incomplete tasks, or *open loops*, from your brain, is robbing you of mental energy.

The Zeigarnik Effect can cost you big in life. The more tasks, decisions, options, thoughts, arguments, to-dos, hopes and dreams you leave unresolved, the more they are taking up space in your brain.

They are being held by your memory, whether it's your working memory, short-term memory, or long-term memory. Either way, this holding pattern of incomplete tasks is using up your mental energy. It's also wreaking havoc on your emotional well-being.

The Zeigarnik Effect is biological; it is unyielding and will consume you if you let it. Studies show that the Zeigarnik Effect can reduce your ability to make decisions;[3] it can lead to intrusive and repetitive negative thoughts,[4] and may play a role in post-traumatic stress, obsessive-compulsive disorder, and general anxiety disorder.[5]

Unresolved issues can dramatically affect not only your energy levels and emotions, but your overall health and well-being as well. You can't stop the Zeigarnik Effect from affecting your brain; however, you can manage it and prevent it from taking control of you by frequently closing your brain's open loops.

How to Start Closing Off Your Brain's Open Loops

Have you ever felt a sense of relief after making a list of things that were on your mind, or after journaling the events that happened to you over the past day, week, month, year? Have you ever felt a sense of relief after cleaning your room, cleaning out your garage, donating all of your old clothes to charity, or finally organizing all of your paper receipts? If so, you've experienced the focus and energy-boosting effects of eliminating your brain's open loops. Purging or elimination is *not* the first step of closing off the open loops in your brain.

Gathering is the first step. Gathering makes elimination possible. You must first identify and gather together all the open loops that are currently draining your mental energy levels and dysregulating your emotions.

These open loops include every piece of incoming information in your physical surroundings and in your memory—from handwritten notes to emails and receipts, to the dirty laundry in the hamper and the dirty dishes in the sink, to the vacation you've always wanted to take, what college your kids will go to, the argument you had last night with your spouse, the traumatic health diagnosis you had five years ago and never recovered from, on and on.

Everything. All of it. You must gather all of this "stuff"—all of these open loops—into one place before you will ever return your focus, mental energy levels, and emotional state back to true normal.

Some of your stuff will be physical (repainting the deck, paper clutter on your desk) and some of it will be virtual (emails, online documents) or psychological (a relationship that ended badly that you never got over, wanting to start a new diet). As a result, you need to create both a giant list (one single extremely long list) and a large pile of stuff.

For most people, this gathering phase takes at least 24 hours of 100% attention.[6] This means you'll need to set aside a day, or even an entire weekend, to just "gather." The most important part of the gathering phase might surprise you: *do not* start eliminating—or, worse, *executing* tasks—as you gather.

Notes

1. Zeigarnik, B. (1927) 'On finished and unfinished business'. http://codeblab.com/wp-content/uploads/2009/12/On-Finished-and-Unfinished-Tasks.pdf

2. Burke, W. W. (2010) 'A perspective on the field of organization development and change: The Zeigarnik effect'. http://journals.sagepub.com/doi/abs/10.1177/0021886310388161

3. Masicampo, E. J. and Baumeister, Roy F. (2011) 'Unfulfilled goals interfere with tasks that require executive functions'. *Journal of Experimental Social Psychology* 47(2): 300–311. http://www.sciencedirect.com/science/article/pii/S0022103110002283

4. Horowitz, M. J. (1975) 'Intrusive and repetitive thoughts after experimental stress'. *Archives of General Psychiatry* 32(11): 1457–1463. http://archpsyc.jamanetwork.com/article.aspx?articleid=491457

5. James, I. A. and Kendell, K. (1997) 'Unfinished processing in the emotional disorders: The Zeigarnik effect'. *Behavioral and Cognitive Psychotherapy*, 25(4): 329–337.

6. Allen, D. (2002) *Getting things done: The art of stress free productivity*. Penguin Books. https://www.amazon.com/Getting-Things-Done-Stress-Free-Productivity/dp/0142000280

11 Keep it and Clarify it, or Delete it From Your Life Completely

Life is really simple, but we insist on making it complicated.

—Confucius

The only thing worse than being too lazy is being too busy. Remember, there's a difference between being busy and being productive. Busy people focus on efficiency and doing as much as possible. Productive people focus on effectiveness and doing the minimum amount possible to achieve the maximum effect.

Effectiveness is your priority, but efficiency is still important. Efficiency allows for effectiveness. To be efficient, you must start systemizing your internal and external environments. But before you can systemize anything, you need to organize it. You need to determine which parts of your would-be system stay and which parts go.

The previous chapter showed you how to identify and gather your brain's open loops. This one will show you how to organize these loops. Before you continue, you must have your open loop list completely done.

All your "stuff" must be in one giant list, whether written in a Microsoft Word document, Google Drive document, or on paper. Ideally, you should have between 100–200 items on your list (this is the average number of open loops each person carries with them on a daily basis).

Now, with your list in hand, you need to organize it. Go through your items with only two options in mind: keep and clarify it, or delete it entirely.

Actively Delete Your Open Loops, Don't Just Passively "Let Go"

Not everything on your list was meant to stay in your life. You will need to delete some things. That may include goals, ideas, projects, and even people that are no longer right for you. You will need to be very deliberate in choosing which open loops you let stay in your life. Your mental energy depends on your deliberation.

The key is to take an active role in eliminating open loops that no longer belong in your life. Do not fall into the trap of "letting go" of them. Letting go is not enough. You need to decide to cut off the open loops that don't matter. The "cis" in the word "de-cis-ion" (and the word "in-cis-ion") comes from its Latin root which means "to cut," as in, to cut off. You must actively decide which open loops to excise from your life.

In looking over your list the first time, quickly determine whether each item should be kept for now and further clarified, or cut out. If you wrote down something during an emotional high or low, or if there is something you instantly know you want gone, delete it from the list. (Don't waste too much time deciding on which items to remove during this first pass.) If an item you wrote down is a keeper or might be a keeper, leave it on the list and clarify it.

During the initial creation of your list, you likely just jotted down a very brief note for each item—some chicken scratch to remind you of what that loop was about. Here is where you make it understandable and actionable by clarifying the end result that you want to be achieved.

How to Make Your Open Loops Actionable

Once you complete the first pass of your list, set it aside for 12–24 hours and then come back to it. Next, go through the list of keepers that you clarified and ask yourself one simple question: "Is it actionable?"

If the answer is YES, then keep it on the list, which I will now refer to as your Actionable list (and put it in your Actionable folder). If the answer is NO, then you need to remove it from the list and either delete it (only if you're sure it will never come into your mind again) or put it on one of two new folders: a Someday folder or a Source folder.

These two folders are *only* for items that are *not* actionable, like a tropical vacation brochure or a blog article on learning to fly airplanes. (These things would go on the Someday folder because you want to get around to it eventually but no concrete action is required or readily available to you right now.) A quick start guide on how to use LinkedIn to get a job or a how-to guide on getting more Facebook fans would go in your Source folder because they are not actionable in themselves but can be used as a Source for something actionable.

These three folders—Actionable, Someday, and Source—are best kept virtually in Word documents within your computer's hard drive folders, Google Drive Documents within Google Drive folders, or similar.

You will want to add an Attachments subfolder within each of your main folders. This will keep the inside of each folder decluttered, with each showing only a prioritized list and an Attachment subfolder containing all documents that are supplementary to the list. You can add links to documents in your Attachment subfolders to your prioritized lists for easy access.

Be sure to backup these folders regularly with a hard drive or cloud storage system. One last folder you will eventually need to add is a Delegation folder. Your Delegation folder will contain a subfolder for each person you're working with on any project. Each of these subfolders should have an Actionable list and an Attachment subfolder belonging to both you and the person you are working with and/or delegating project items.

Now that your brain's open loops are gathered, clarified, and organized, and now that you've learned how to be selective by eliminating energy-depleting emotions, events, and people from your life, you have the tools and mental space necessary to start systemizing your internal and external environments.

Recall that this systemization process relies on both self-regulation and the scientific concept of "automaticity."

The rest of this book will focus on how to systematically and scientifically leverage the power of creative ownership and pragmatic growth. Specifically, you will learn how to stop being dependent on other people for your personal and professional success. Instead, you will learn how to start investing in your own individual supply of knowledge, network, and ability.

Case Study #2: Yuri Klyachkin, PhD

"Here's your unemployment check, Doctor."

Yuri Klyachkin was about to be unemployed for the second time.

Like a lot of graduate students, Yuri transitioned into a postdoctoral position, or postdoc, after getting his PhD in microbiology. Postdocs are low-paying training positions that are supposed to prepare you for becoming a professor in academia.

The problem is that professorships have declined sharply in the last four decades. Now, only 0.45% of PhDs will ever become a professor. The rest transition into non-academic careers or stay in academia doing multiple postdocs. The academic landscape is so rough for PhDs now that between 60 and 80% of all PhDs will become unemployed or stuck in postdocs.

Such was Yuri's fate. Yuri was in the middle of his third year as a postdoc when the lab he was working for ran out of funding. Just like that, Yuri was out of a job.

That's right—a highly skilled PhD with postdoc experience had to go on unemployment.

Imagine going to school for 30 years, doing highly technical work as a microbiologist, and having to show up at the unemployment office. Imagine having to sit there embarrassed and angry while someone asks you, "Did you apply for four jobs this week?"

Imagine being highly skilled and highly motivated but treated like you are lazy—like you are a loser. Imagine having to go home to your family and tell them the last 30 years were a waste.

After six months of unemployment, Yuri found another lab that was looking for a postdoc. So, Yuri agreed to do another. Now, nearly three years later (again), Yuri was about to be unemployed for the second time. This was when Yuri decided to change his perspective and change his strategy.

Yuri, as he describes it, had "special snowflake syndrome." He thought that because he had a PhD that he shouldn't have to apply for a job. Instead, a job should just be given to him. This "syndrome" was passed down to him by others in academia. Lifetime academics had told Yuri that he would be a failure if he left the university system. They told Yuri that he couldn't do "real science" outside of it.

The first step Yuri took to changing his situation was to stop listening to these unsolicited opinions. Then he started carving time out of his day to execute a high-level job search. Yuri still had to finish his work in the lab and take care of his family. Despite these obligations, he had found a way to start sending out targeted résumés, networking with employers, and setting up interviews.

To accomplish this, Yuri kept a simple daily journal and marked in it when his mental energy levels were high and when they were low. By doing this, he discovered that his mental energy levels peaked in the morning from 7:30 a.m. to 9:30 a.m. local time. To take advantage of this time for his biggest priority, getting a job, Yuri started waking up earlier so he could work on his job search prior to going into the lab. He went to the university library and, first, created a list of everything he needed to do to get a job. Then he made a list of everything that was distracting him from accomplishing this goal. Next, Yuri consolidated his lists by eliminating everything that wasn't in one of three categories—family, finishing lab experiments, and getting a new job.

At this point, Yuri turned his attention entirely to the "getting a new job category" and set up two folders on his desktop: "Actionable" and "Source." Yuri organized all of his job leads into the Source folder and all of the tasks he needed to execute related to these leads in his Actionable folder. After collecting leads and listing actions for a week, Yuri started executing.

Two weeks later, he was hired as Medical Science Liaison at Bristol-Myers-Squibb making $100,000 (~£76,000) a year. Just nine months after that, Yuri was promoted into a management role at Celgene as a Regional Science Liaison, making even more money.

After getting hired, Yuri realized that his PhD never lost its value; he just was too busy and too distracted to leverage it. He won't ever make that mistake again, and he spends part of his time encouraging other PhDs not to make it either.

Part 2
Creative
Ownership

The individual has always had to struggle to keep from being overwhelmed by the tribe. To be your own man is a hard business. If you try it, you'll be lonely often, and sometimes frightened. But no price is too high to pay for the privilege of owning yourself.

—Rudyard Kipling

Creative ownership relieves you of dependence. Everything in your life can be taken away from you except for your knowledge, network, and ability. Gaining ownership over these three things will accelerate your progress on the path to *Intelligent Achievement*. Failing to gain ownership, however, will ensure that you are only ever one bad phone call away from disaster.

12 Where Millennials and Baby Boomers Meet

Investing in yourself is the best investment you will ever make.
it will not only improve your life, it will improve the lives of all
those around you.

—Robin Sharma

If you read Part 1 of this book and have started to implement its selectivity-based strategies, you are now on the path to *Intelligent Achievement*. You've likely already noticed a remarkable increase in your mental energy levels.

At this point, you're likely asking yourself, *What now?*

Where do I invest this extra energy?

The answer is in creative ownership.

But ownership of what? Should you go out and buy a new car? How about a new handbag or watch? Should you learn to play the stock market, or book a cabana on AirBnB and fly to some remote island to lounge for two months?

When it comes to creative ownership, there are two predominant philosophies today.

The first philosophy has been popularized over the past ten years by a slew of books and media in general advocating for a material-free lifestyle and simultaneously calling for the death of office work.

This "experience" philosophy has coincided with the rise of the *Millennial* generation, which includes individuals born between 1977 and 1997, and states that you should live a short-term-oriented lifestyle despite the fact that you will likely live a very long time. It says that you should own experiences over material possessions, and you should not wait until you retire to start living like a retiree (because you will likely never stop working).

Companies like Facebook (virtual friends), Upwork (virtual workers), AirBnB (temporary house ownership), and Uber (temporary car ownership) are all the result of this philosophy. Terms like "side hustle," "content marketing," and "entre-employment" (see the next chapter) are the result of this philosophy as well.

The experience philosophy leans on data showing that you will live and work a long time (and you'll work at 7+ different jobs throughout your life) so you should not waste your time investing in a retirement plan, buying a house, building up long-term assets, and so on. Instead, you should invest in mobility, liquidity, and options, because these are the only things worth owning in today's world.

This is an alluring stance especially considering that 91% of Millennials expect to stay in a job for less than three years, according to a *Future Workplace* survey of 1,189 employees and 150 managers. If this holds true, these Millennials will have 15–20 jobs over the course of their working lives.[1]

The second philosophy states that you should invest for the long term only.

This "equity" philosophy gained popularity in the years following World War II, when there was a temporary marked increase in the birth rate. People born during this time were labeled as *Baby Boomers* and were told to save, store, prepare, and plan.

Boomers were encouraged to buy a moderately priced house and live in it for 30 or more years to gain equity. They were told to invest in a single career to get retirement benefits and better healthcare. They were also told to diversify their investments, which meant investing in stocks, bonds, startups, gold bullions, and material status symbols that will help them get recognized, promoted, and connected.

This Boomer perspective says you should spend your 20s, 30s, and 40s paying into your investments, professional reputation, image, status, and personal empire because these things collectively equal success and because you're not going to have the time (or the stamina) to build this kind of equity in your 50s, 60s, and 70s.

Both of these philosophies are riddled with faults and misconceptions, but both are also built on solid premises and can culminate into a happy and successful life. My question is, "Why can't you have both?" This should be your question too.

How Experience and Equity Combine to Create True Value

True value is based on experience and equity, not one or the other. This is true no matter what decision you are considering, financial or otherwise. Experience is simply something that you are involved in; it's engaging with and/or observing facts or events.

In the fields of business and finance, equity can refer to stock or any other security representing an ownership interest.[2] It can also refer to a company's balance sheet, the amount of the funds contributed by the owners (the stockholders) plus the retained earnings (or losses).

In the context of real estate, equity can refer to the difference between the current fair market value of the property and the amount the owner still owes on the mortgage. Here, we are referring to equity as anything you've invested in that has *earned* value.

The problem is that most people judge value, especially financial value, by either experience or equity. For example, people who choose to spend their entire savings on vacation after vacation without ever holding down a steady job are focused only on experience.

They spend their money on these experiences but, after the trips are over, have nothing to show for them but memories and pictures. In other words, they have no earned value.

They didn't learn anything. They didn't increase their network. They just partied.

Other people never go on a vacation and instead pinch every single penny. They never go out for coffee. They never travel. They just save. As a result, they have more financial security—they have more equity—but they have earned this value through creating an experience deficit.

If you're living for experiences only, you're equity-poor. If you're living for equity only, you're experience-poor. Either way, you're poor and being poor, always leads to dependence. The only way to truly relieve yourself of dependence in life is to start collecting both experiences and equity at the same time.

Experiences That Create Equity and Wealth

Becoming an owner in today's world and today's economy is a two-step strategy. The first step is to start filling your life with experiences that create equity for you and, as a result, generate more ownership for you. The second is to systemize and automate your ownership by filling other people's lives with experiences that create equity for them.

The more ownership-building systems you create and automate for yourself and others, the more mental energy you will free up and the more purpose and adventure you will be able to add to your life.

The first step to true ownership is simple once you understand which types of experiences create real equity. The world has changed dramatically over the past 30 years. You used to need an entire factory and storefront property to start a business. Now, all you need is an internet connection.

A kid in India with a cell phone has a more powerful computer than the U.S. President had in the 1960s. (It's true—your iPhone is millions of times more powerful than all of NASA's combined computing in 1969.)[3] Things are different.

Equity is different too, and today there are only three forms of equity: *knowledge, network,* and *ability.* The bank can take everything else away from you, everything but your knowledge, network, and ability.

Start investing in experiences that expand your knowledge base, grow your network, and increase your abilities. Do you ever wonder how some of the world's most successful people go bankrupt over and over again and remain on top (or end up on top again shortly after their downfall)? The reason they rebound so quickly is that they've invested heavily in their knowledge, network, and ability.

Experiences that build real equity will not only make you less dependent on others for success; they will make you less dependent on others for happiness too. A national survey of 12,000 people found that experiential purchases make people happier than material purchases.[4]

Other studies confirm that experiences carry more monetary value than material items.[5] Of course, our goal is for you to have everything: experience, equity, wealth, and all the material goods you want. But sequence matters. You need to become an owner first. You need to invest in the right equity and equity-building experiences first.

Notes

1. Meister, J. (2012) 'The future of work: Job hopping is the new normal for millennials'. *Forbes.* https://www.forbes.com/forbes/welcome/?toURL=https://www.forbes.com/sites/jeannemeister/2012/08/14/the-future-of-work-job-hopping-is-the-new-normal-for-millennials/&refURL=&referrer=#2c5db39013b8

2. 'Equity'. Investopedia. http://www.investopedia.com/terms/e/equity.asp

3. 'Your smartphone is millions of times more powerful than all of NASA's combined computing in 1969'. *AME Science*. http://www.zmescience.com/research/technology/smartphone-power-compared-to-apollo-432/

4. 'Experiences make people happier than material goods, says University of Colorado prof.' *Science Daily*. https://www.sciencedaily.com/releases/2004/12/041219182811.htm

5. Pchelin, P. and Howell, R. T. (2012) 'The hidden cost of value-seeking: People do not accurately forecast the economic benefits of experiential purchases'. *The Journal of Positive Psychology*, 9(4). http://www.tandfonline.com/doi/full/10.1080/17439760.2014.898316#.U4EAg1hdUmc

13 "Entre-Employee" and Temp-Employee are the Only Career Options Left

A few weeks ago I visited a friend of mine who manages a trillion dollars. No joke. A trillion. If I told you the name of the family he worked for you would say, "they have a trillion? Really?" But that's what happens when ten million dollars compounds at 2% over 200 years.

He said, "look out the windows." We looked out at all the office buildings around us. "What do you see?" he said. "I don't know." "They're empty! All the cubicles are empty. The middle class is being hollowed out." And I took a closer look. Entire floors were dark. Or there were floors with one or two cubicles but the rest empty. "It's all outsourced or technology has taken over for the paper shufflers," he said.

"Not all the news is bad," he said. "More people entered the upper class than ever last year." "But," he said, "more people are temp staffers than ever."

—James Altucher

If you think your employer is loyal to you, try getting sick for a few months in a row. The average U.S. employee only gets two weeks of paid vacation and three weeks of unpaid medical leave.[1] The numbers are much better for U.K. employees at 28 vacation days a year,[2] but this may be changing now that the U.K. is no longer part of the European Union. (The E.U. in 1993 required all member countries to set a minimum of 20 days of paid vacation days per year.)

Regardless of the number of vacation days you have, don't you want more? Why not have 100 days of vacation. Or 200? Or 365? The real question is, *Are you required to do what your employer tells you to do?*

Are you dependent on your employer?

If so, how does it feel to be dependent?

No matter where you work, it's relatively easy for any company to let go of any employee they don't want around anymore. Sure, some countries have rigorous wrongful firing laws, but when money is involved, there's always a loophole.

Personally, I don't see anything wrong with this. No one else is responsible for your success, just like no one else is responsible for your happiness or health. If you have allowed yourself to be dependent on any one entity or any one person for your survival (as I did), then it's your fault (just like it was my fault).

Given how little vacation the average employee gets compared to how much time they spend working, and given how many jobs the average employee will have over their lifetime—not to mention how easily any employee can lose their job—everyone has become a temporary employee.

If you are working for only one employer and doing nothing on the side, you are still a temporary employee. You are expendable. Don't believe me? The numbers don't lie. In the U.S. the recession of 2008 killed off 7.9 million jobs,[3] most of which never came back. At the end of 2008 in the U.K., unemployment rose to 1,860,000 and, by March 2009, increased to more than 2 million—the highest level the nation had seen for more than 12 years.

By April 2010, U.K. unemployment exceeded 2.5 million for the first time in 16 years.[4] When the going gets tough for a company, no matter the cause, you will be let go. This is something I experienced firsthand.

A few years ago, I had a health scare, and while I was still recovering from emergency surgery, the company I was working for told me they couldn't extend my medical leave. That's when I realized I was expendable and in trouble. I did the math and realized I was only a couple of months away from being completely broke.

Fortunately, I had started a blog and published a book that did well the year before, so I was going to be able to pay my bills a bit longer. But this *bit* ran out too. How did I get here? I was very successful for my age. I was doing far better than other people my age.

Wasn't I? I mean, I had carefully crafted an online image of myself as successful and had thousands of blog readers and Facebook fans because of it. How could someone like me be about to lose it all?

That's when I realized there's a big difference between fake success and *Intelligent Achievement*. That's when I realized I had spent years as nothing more than a temporary employee doing what temps do best: protecting my image and chasing job titles above all else.

Eventually, I realized I needed to stop being dependent and start being an owner.

But how?

What was the path to ownership?

How could I stop being temporarily employed? What was on the other side of temp-employment? The answer, I learned, was *entre-employment*.

What Is an *Entre*-Employee?

Entre-employees are the new upper class. Demand for entrepreneurship and innovation are at an all-time high in both the U.S.[5] and the U.K.[6] This makes sense because self-employed people make up nearly three-fourths of all millionaires in the world.[7]

Business owners, including online business owners, comprise 74% of all millionaires in the U.S. and 43% of all millionaires in the U.K.[8] Senior executives, such as company CEOs and CFOs like Tim Cook (Apple) or John Mackey (Whole Foods) make up 10%. Doctors, lawyers, and

other people with advanced degrees make up another 10%.
Salespeople and consultants make up 5%, and the remaining
1% belongs to stockbrokers, inventors, actors, directors,
authors, songwriters, athletes, and lottery winners.

Here's the kicker: most of these entrepreneurs used to
work for someone else. This means that before these millionaires were entrepreneurs, they were entre-employees.
They started their businesses (or at the very least developed
their business model and plan) while working at their day job.
And guess what? *Today's employers are encouraging you to do
this too.*

Why Employers Want to Hire Entrepreneurs

It might sound confusing, but employers like to see some
entrepreneurial spirit in their employees, even though they
are hiring them to work for the company. This does not
mean that they want you to quit immediately and start your
own business, but they do want you to demonstrate some
of the necessary attributes to work independently and take
responsibility for your work.

Employers value employees who are capable of performing without needing to be continuously supervised. They want
employees who perform with minimum supervision but know
when to ask for explicit instruction. They also value employees
who can respond maturely when confronted with unexpected
challenges.

Employees who use creative problem-solving skills to find
new solutions for unexpected hurdles are more likely to thrive
in challenging work environments, and employers know it.

That is why many of the world's top organizations, such as Google and 3M allow employees to spend up to 20% of their work hours doing whatever they want.

In *Planet Entrepreneur*, author Steve Strauss calls attention to the fact that the growth of many corporate giants, including Apple, Intel, Lockheed-Martin, Toyota, and as mentioned earlier Google and 3M.[9] It was an entre-employee at 3M who accidentally discovered Post-it notes by playing with adhesives, and it was entre-employees at Google who developed Gmail and Google News.

Why The Temp-Employee Class is Growing Exponentially

While the upper class continues to grow linearly, the bottom class continues to grow exponentially. There were *more* people below the poverty line in the U.S.[10] and U.K. in 2015 than any other year since 1959.

That's right—more people are in poverty today in many of the world's most developed countries than ever. In the U.K., the number of people living in poverty is now over 21% and climbing.[11]

On top of this, more people are *under*employed than ever before. In 2016, 51% of Millennials report being underemployed, compared to 41% in 2013. What's happening?

People who refuse to be entre-employees will be left behind, no matter how much they want to better their lives. Consider this: according to Marketdata Enterprises, during the recession of 2008, English-speaking countries spent more than

$11 billion on self-improvement books, CDs, seminars, coaching and stress-management programs.[12] This is 13.6% more than they spent in 2005.

The latest forecasts show that this growth will continue through 2020, and not just in the U.S. and the U.K. Countries like China and India have started to dive deeply into the personal development industry.[13] Yet, despite the billions spent on self-help, current numbers show that most people are less happy today than they were in 2011.[14]

In fact, one study shows that most people are less happy today than they were 30 years ago.[15] Other research also shows that people are growing up less mentally tough and resilient than they used to be and that the average person is having less fun now than he used to at work.[16] Why is all of this self-help not helping?

The temp-employee class is growing exponentially (and helplessly) for two reasons. First, temp-employees do work they don't enjoy and never start anything of their own. As a result, they are perpetual dependents. Instead of owning anything of value in their life, such as a broad knowledge base, a deep network, and a diverse skill set, they remain completely dependent on others for their success and happiness. Second, they spend all their time, energy, and money (especially money they don't have) trying to derive a sense of ownership from material objects and other people.

A survey of 2,500 people showed that 87% of people are happier living with fewer possessions.[17] Yet very few people are opting to live with less. The reason so many people are unhappy is that they are stuffing their lives full of useless possessions and unhealthy relationships. Credit card debt is on the rise again with the average household owing more than $7,000.[18]

One in 11 households owns self-storage space—an increase of 75% from 1995. In the U.K., there are approximately 37.6 million square feet of self-storage space, and the total turnover of the industry in 2015 was £440 million.[19] In the U.S., there are now over 40,000 self-storage facilities; these self-storage numbers are increasing.[20]

Finding Creative Ownership in Entre-Employment

Ownership creates happiness and employees who engage in entrepreneurial pursuits have a greater sense of purpose than any other category of worker. Surveys show that 97% of entrepreneurs feel a sense of purpose on a daily basis while only 25% of full-time or part-time workers (temp-employees) feel a sense of purpose.

Other survey data has shown that over 70% of employees are "not engaged" or "actively disengaged" from their jobs.[21] Ownership is what makes people feel engaged in their work and their lives outside the office.

Scientific research shows that, without a sense of ownership, people are more likely to quit what they are doing. In fact, people without a sense of ownership are more likely to quit on life. One scientific study showed that early retirees who completely lose their sense of ownership and purpose are 65% more likely to die before the age of 60 than those who do not retire early.[22]

The only way to avoid disengagement in your work (and maybe even an early death) is to avoid becoming a permanent temp-employee and instead, enter the world of entre-employment.

Entre-employment, or the relationship between entrepreneurship and employment in your own life, can take several forms. You can build up your business while you're at your current job and then jump ship once your business is self-sustaining.

You can make a personal project profitable and then cut a deal with your employer so that both they and you benefit from it. You can negotiate a deal with a new company that allows you to run your own consulting company or small business while working for them. These are just a few of many possible examples.

As long as you stay transparent and creative, you and your employer can benefit from this new entre-employee model.

In the following section of this book, you will learn strategies for leveraging your new entre-employee mindset to relieve yourself of dependence. You will learn how to create automated streams of income for yourself and/or for you and your employer.

You will learn the principles of content creation, content marketing, and scaling up a personal and professional platform. These principles will lead to increased amounts of experience-based equity in your life and decreased levels of dependence. At the end of this section, you will have the tools you need to sustain high levels of ownership while continuing to make progress on the path to *Intelligent Achievement*.

Notes

1. BLS. Economic news release. Table 5. 'Average paid holidays and days of vacation and sick leave for full-time employees'. https://www.bls.gov/news.release/ebs.t05.htm

2. Sherter, A. (2013) 'When it comes to vacations, the U.S. stinks'. *Moneywatch*. http://www.cbsnews.com/news/when-it-comes-to-vacations-the-us-stinks/

3. Isidore, C. (2010) '7.9 million jobs lost—many forever'. *CNN Money*. http://money.cnn.com/2010/07/02/news/economy/jobs_gone_forever/index.htm

4. 'UK unemployment increases to 2.5 million'. *BBC News*. http://news.bbc.co.uk/2/hi/8634241.stm

5. Pofeldt, E. (2013) 'US entrepreneurship hits record high'. *Forbes*. https://www.forbes.com/sites/elainepofeldt/2013/05/27/u-s-entrepreneurship-hits-record-high/#16b0d6451d79

6. Payne, C. (2016) 'UK entrepreneurial performance at all-time high, according to index'. *London School of Business and Finance*. http://www.lsbf.org.uk/blog/news/enterpreneurs-startups/uk-entrepreneurial-performance-all-time-high-index/108372

7. Miller, D. (2009) 'No more dreaded Mondays: Ignite your passion and other revolutionary ways to find your true calling at work'. https://www.amazon.com/No-More-Dreaded-Mondays-Revolutionary/dp/0307588777

8. 'Most millionaires are self-employed'. AskMen.com. http://uk.askmen.com/top_10/money/becoming-a-millionaire_5.html

9. Strauss, S. (2013) *Planet Entrepreneur*. John Wiley & Sons. https://www.amazon.com/Planet-Entrepreneur-Entrepreneurship-Business-Success/dp/1118789520

10. Basic statistics. Talk Poverty. https://talkpoverty.org/basics/

11. Gov.uk. 'Households below average income: 1994/95 to 2014/15' https://www.gov.uk/government/statistics/households-below-average-income-199495-to-201415

12. PRWeb. '$10.4 Billion self-improvement market survives scandals & recession'. http://www.prweb.com/releases/2013/1/prweb10275905.htm

13. MinistryofTofu. 'Help yourself China: The rise of self-help culture and its unique Chinese features'. http://www.ministryoftofu.com/2012/04/help-yourself-china-the-rise-of-self-help-culture-and-its-unique-chinese-features/

14. Yang, M. (2013) 'Poll: Americans are less happy now than they were in 2011'. *Time*. http://newsfeed.time.com/2013/06/02/poll-americans-are-less-happy-now-than-they-were-in-2011/

15. Reuters. (2007) 'Americans less happy today than 30 years ago: study'. http://www.reuters.com/article/us-happiness-usa-idUSL1550309820070615

16. HuffingtonUK. (2013) 'Resilient youth: Using psychology to prevent a lost generation'. http://www.huffingtonpost.co.uk/ed-pinkney/psychology-to-prevent-lost-generation_b_3372057.html

17. Alexander, S. and Ussher, S. (2011) 'The voluntary simplicity movement: A multi-national survey analysis in theoretical context'. http://simplicityinstitute.org/wp-content/uploads/2011/04/The-Voluntary-Simplicity-Movement-Report-11a.pdf

18. Grant, K. (2014) 'Rising credit card debt may dampen holiday budgets'. CNBC. http://www.cnbc.com/2014/09/11/rising-credit-card-debt-may-dampen-holiday-budgets.html

19. SSA. 'Size of the industry'. https://www.ssauk.com/industry-info/size-of-the-industry/

20. Pruitt, A. D. (2013) 'Self-storage gains cachet as values rise'. *Wall Street Journal*. https://www.wsj.com/articles/SB10001424127887323764804578314282995510800

21. C. Gallo. (2011) '70% of your employees hate their jobs'. *Forbes*. https://www.forbes.com/sites/carminegallo/2011/11/11/your-emotionally-disconnected-employees/#60c44e042d5c

22. Tsai, S. *et al.* (2005) 'Age at retirement and long term survival of an industrial population: prospective cohort study'. *BMJ. 331*:995. http://www.bmj.com/content/331/7523/995

14 Content Marketing Is Creative Ownership

Content is king.

—Bill Gates

In the past, motivated employees who wanted to earn extra income and/or become less dependent on a single source of income would take on a second job at a second company. In other words, they would moonlight.

Moonlighting simply refers to having a second job in addition to one's regular employment.

Most moonlighters would get a second job at a call center, restaurant, or somewhere else where the hours were either evening shift, night shift, or at least flexible. The problem is that for the motivated employee, moonlighting meant being out of the house and away from family.

This would put a significant strain on the employee's home life and relationships. As a result, traditional moonlighting is an exhausting, and often destructive, way to get ahead professionally.

Enter *content marketing*.

As mentioned in the previous chapter, the internet now provides a way for motivated employees, or "entre-employees" to generate a second income while still working at their current job. This second income stream could come in the form of consulting calls, book and eBook sales, informational products, physical products, membership programs, and much more.

The advantage of these types of income stream is that they can be both created and delivered from your home. Thanks to the internet, you can make a personal project profitable very quickly by working in the evenings and weekends—from wherever you want.

The key, once again, is following the right sequence. When it comes to infusing your life with selectivity and ownership, sequence is everything.

A question that you might be asking now is: "Why do I need to generate *additional streams of income?*"

Besides the obvious answers of becoming more financially independent and more location independent, the reason you want to create additional streams of income is so you can conserve more of your mental energy, which will allow you to become even more selective with your attention and effort.

Ideally, the streams of income you create should be automated as quickly as possible. Once they are automated, you will be in a position to earn income passively. This kind of passive income is what will allow you to live a more free, full, and adventurous life. Of course, this is not an easy process. On the contrary, it's a highly specific process, one that must be followed exactly.

Failing to follow the right sequence is where most people get tripped up. For example, a common mistake most new "entre-employees" make when building up their first passive income stream is by spending all of their resources on social media.

These people falsely believe that Facebook *likes* and Twitter *retweets* are the starting point of content marketing and generating a second income stream. In reality, these vanity analytics are irrelevant; and social media marketing, in general, is one of the last things they should be focusing on.

If you want to create a passive income stream, you must start with content marketing. Content marketing is the first and arguably most important step in the sequential process of becoming a successful entre-employee.

What is Content Marketing?

In today's world, all media is content marketing.

Every radio show or podcast you listen to, every book or blog article you read, every movie, TV show, or news program you watch—it's all content marketing.

Content marketing is the means by which everyone in the world vies to own the world's most valuable resource—*attention*.

Therefore, *content marketing is ownership*.

On a more practical level, content marketing is a strategic marketing approach focused on creating and distributing valuable, relevant, and consistent content to attract and retain the attention of an audience.

On an even more practical level, content marketing is a means by which individuals and businesses convert readers, users, and viewers into buyers. Most often this is done by first turning audience members into longtime subscribers by building trust. Here, trust is established by creating high-quality content and delivering it consistently.

Today, most individuals and businesses' favorite mode of content delivery is a *blog,* a truncation of *web-log*, that used just to describe a discussion or informational site published on the World Wide Web. Now, blogging refers more specifically to a regularly updated website or web page that is written in an informal or conversational style, whether run by an individual or business.

Blogging is arguably the most effective means of communicating content to an audience quickly, directly, and cheaply.

You cannot be a successful entre-employee without blogging. Teaching is the new advertising and blogging is your means of teaching people why they should care about what you're doing. Blogging is also the first step to gaining ownership over an audience's attention, which is the starting point of all successful ventures in today's world.

15 Leveraging Walt Disney's Secret System of Creativity

The way to get started is to quit talking and begin doing.

—Walt Disney

Content marketing in the form of a blog is the most effective way to find out who your ideal audience is, and what they're interested in. It's also an effective way to figure out what interests you.

The problem is many people *hate* to write.

This hatred, however, often stems from nothing more than a misunderstanding of the content creation process.

Creating content is not magic, even though the barriers to successful content creation can seem supernatural. While writer's block, freezing up in front of a camera, and falling asleep on an empty palette are almost proverbial, the good news is that creation is a science, which means there's a method to its madness.

One method, in particular, has been shown over and over again to be highly effective when it comes to creating content: the Disney Method. Scientific studies have shown that the Disney method[1] is one of the most effective ways to come up with high-quality content. Not only has the Disney Method been shown to be a very effective way for an individual to create quality content; it has also been shown to be a highly effective way for groups to do it too.

When it comes to creating content, the most important (and tough) lesson to learn is how to keep your internal editor turned off. If you've written anything in the past, you've probably noticed a little voice in your head reading and rereading what you were writing as you were writing it, telling you that it was awful.

- "That last sentence was horrible!"
- "Wow, you are the world's worst writer!"
- "You're like Ernest Hemingway's untalented sober twin!"

Everyone who writes has this internal editor. Without it, you wouldn't be able to write quality content. Your internal editor holds you to a higher standard and helps you find and correct mistakes.

But, you must control your internal editor. You must only turn your editor on AFTER you've written the first draft of your content.

Writing with your internal editor turned off is called the *creative*, or *dreamer* phase.

During this phase, you should write with reckless abandon. Write as if no one will ever read your draft. Step into your freest, most creative self and just write what comes into your mind.

That also means that you write without worrying about spelling or grammar. It could mean that you use cuss words. It could be that you write with a lighter tone, an angrier tone, or a playful, sarcastic, enlightened, crass, or excited tone. The key is to do what comes naturally and just let it pour out.

This is the *realistic* phase, and it's where you turn your internal editor back on. However, your internal editor should only be turned on halfway.

The goal at this point is to edit your first draft loosely. Look to correct the broad strokes. Does this paragraph make sense here or should it be moved further down the page?

Can someone else read this and make sense of it at all? How much of their mental energy would need to be devoted to *figuring out what you're trying to say* versus simply consuming it? If you went off on some crazy tangent midway through the article, delete it. Again, your aim is to put the big pieces together so that it flows somewhat logically.

The third and final step is to rip apart your writing critically. This is called the *critical* step, and the goal is to ruthlessly cut all the fat out of your second draft. This is where you're going to go through every sentence, line by line, and you're going to slash and burn every word that doesn't need to be there. Editor voice can be cranked up to full volume.

Get rid of every single "that" or "in other words" or "as a result" that doesn't absolutely need to be there. Blogs are skimmed, not read, so make sure your text is super tight. Remember, this is the very last step. It's at the opposite side of the spectrum from the creative phase. First, you're creative, then you're realistic, and then you're critical. This process must be followed *sequentially* in order to protect your audience's mental energy levels.

What You Should Write (or, Overcoming Writer's Block)

Writer's block comes to those who refuse to write what they know. You've lived, you have stories, you've learned skills—this is what you should start writing about. To start, just sit down and start writing about what happened to you yesterday.

Then write about something that happened to you as a kid. Then write about a skill you learned in high school or college, or something you learned about during one of your first jobs or your current job.

Get used to writing about what you've experienced. Then get used to summarizing other people's experiences and forming opinions. Read an article related to something you enjoy or something you do professionally and summarize it into a short paragraph.

Form an opinion on the article and write it as if you're telling someone else what to do or what not to do. Don't worry about writing articles centered around your business yet. Instead, get in the habit of writing stories, summarizing references, and asserting opinions.

In the chapters that follow, the ideal structure of your blog articles will be discussed, including when, where, and how to tell stories, where to add references, and how to translate informed opinions into actionable takeaways.

For now, just start writing. Get your ideas down on paper because, regardless of what your projects are or what you will eventually try to sell, content is what will grow and sell it. Content is how you're going to spread your message, and it's how you're going to bring people to your platform, to your ideas, and eventually to your product.

Video Blogs are Not Just for the Writing Impaired

Video blogging and blogging are very similar. You'll want to follow the Disney Method and you'll want to practice telling stories, summarizing, and forming opinions.

The biggest difference between video blogging and blogging is that the former requires you to show your face.

Sitting down in front of a camera is very difficult for some people, even if no one else is watching. This is okay; it's a normal reaction. Don't let the very common feeling of being camera shy stop you from video blogging. Studies show that video advertising is 600% more effective than print and direct mail combined.[2]

Studies also found that, before reading any text on a website, 60% of people will watch a video if one is available.

Whether you're sharing a written article with the world for the first time, or you're sharing a short video of yourself for the first time, it will be awkward. But like anything, you'll get used to it with practice.

The key is to follow the Disney Method. Step into that first creative phase with your internal editor completely turned off.

Talk to the camera as though no one will ever, ever see it. If you still feel self-conscious, try this: actively try to make the world's most awkward, horrible video. Try to be bad. Seriously, create an awful video. Act as weird as possible and look as disturbing as possible. This will relax you.

By playing out your worst-case scenario, you'll re-anchor yourself in reality. It works.

Once you get the kinks out, enter the *creative phase* mentally, step in front of the camera, and just talk openly about anything you're passionate about. Talk about the things that really matter to you.

Tell a funny story.

Talk about what happened the day before, ten days ago, or even ten years ago.

Talk about something you read or watched recently.

Talk about the skills you're interested in learning.

Talk about your business and why it's important.

Next, flip the camera around and watch what you did. Step into the *realistic phase* and analyze the broad strokes of your video.

What came off well? Did you mention any good teaching points? Note the best parts and then organize your notes so you can reshoot the video.

This second shoot will be much easier. You'll notice your words flow better and the message is tighter.

To start, aim to make your videos only 30–90 seconds. This is for two reasons; first, studies show that most people stop watching online videos after 90 seconds[3] and, second, you want to get in the habit of consolidating your thoughts.

Finally, watch the second version of your video, this time with your critical eye. Step into the critical phase and ruthlessly evaluate your video.

Which words, phrases, and sentences can you cut out completely? Where can you trim off a few seconds? Try to tighten up the script. Then, reshoot the video one last time. If you follow the Disney Method and shoot your video three times, the result will be concise and compelling. As a result, your audience's trust in you will grow and, in turn, the size of your audience will grow.

The Disney Method will ensure that you're protecting your audience's mental energy levels by not being confusing or overly clever in the content you create. The more you protect your audience's attention, the more of their attention they will reward you with in the future. Slowly, their trust in you will grow. As a result, they will freely give you more and more of their most valuable asset.

Notes

1. Tausch, S. (2015) 'Thinking like Disney: Supporting the Disney method using ambient feedback based on group performance'. https://www.medien.ifi.lmu.de/pubdb/publications/pub/tausch2015interact/tausch2015interact.pdf

2. 'Just the stats: The science of video engagement'. *SingleGrain*. https://www.singlegrain.com/video-marketing/just-stats-science-video-engagement/

3. Ibid.

16 Finding Your Voice and Letting the Right Audience Pick You

A loud voice cannot compete with a clear voice, even if it's a whisper.

—Barry Neil Kauffman

C ontent marketing is your means of gaining creative ownership over your audience's attention, which could mean driving traffic to a website or to a storefront to get more customers, or driving traffic to your LinkedIn page to get more job offers.

Content marketing is also your means of teaching people why they should care about you and your professional goals (or any goals for that matter). It's also your way of getting feedback on what other people care about, want, and need, whether these people be potential clients, hiring managers, recruiters, referrals, or team members.

If you want attention, whether you're an individual interested in creating a second stream of income, or the head of a business interested in increasing your company's revenue, content marketing is the fastest and most effective way of achieving your goal. For example, top companies that published sixteen or more blog posts per month got four times as many customer leads than companies that published between zero and four monthly posts.[1] This is because properly executed content marketing is 10X more effective for lead conversion than any other forms of marketing.[2]

A critical part of getting and leveraging attention is connecting with other people. Content is only valuable because it is a means of connecting with others. Content is what will allow you to get feedback from the people you're connected with and build stronger and better relationships with your target audience.

The best way to connect with someone is to uncover what drives him or her. What are his interests? What makes her happy? What drives him to take action? What causes her pain? What problems can you solve for him?

But, how can you find out the answers to these questions if you've never met the other person?

The answer is by testing content. Testing content is the most useful way to find out more about your target audience, which will allow you to build a stronger connection with them.

When you test content, you not only measure the material itself, you also test the audience. By writing different types of blog articles, you will be able to see who your readers truly are by what they engage with most.

You can write an article about massage therapists, engineers, corporate recruiters, school teachers, or people who buy lawn ornaments. You can also determine how these people identify themselves by using different keywords. For example, do your audience see themselves as masseuses, massage therapists, or massage professionals?

Creating content is the testing process, and it never stops. By continually creating content, you can learn more and more about who is your target audience. You can also build deeper and deeper levels of trust with this audience, which again, will result in them giving you more and more of their most valuable asset—*attention*.

What's the Message of Your Content?

Creating and testing content allows you to build stronger connections; it also allows you to hone in on the message of your content.

Without a strong message, your content will lose energy quickly and, more importantly, *you* will lose energy quickly. Think about the times your boss asks you to do something without fully explaining it, or something that you are naturally horrible at, or something that is a complete waste of time—empty, pointless work. How does this make you feel? Do you feel full of energy or completely drained?

I'm guessing it's the latter, and the reason why is because the work you've been asked to do is meaningless. There's no great reason, or greater message behind it. As a result, it's completely misaligned with you, your goals, and your expectations.

So, now that you understand the importance of having a message—*what is your message*?

What do you love writing about? Or, what do you love talking about in front of a camera? What do you love teaching? The best way to figure these questions out is through trial and error, or by creating a lot of content. Once you know what you want and what you love to do, you can align it with something you're good at and something there's an actual need for. Once you have these things aligned, you can ask why.

Why do you love what you do, why are you good at it, and why are you doing it at all? By finding solid answers to these questions, you will start to hone in on your message.

Then, all that will be left to do is to align your message with an audience who resonates with your message. The important thing to remember here is that creating content is your best means of discovering both your ideal audience and your message.

Finding Your Voice in a Noisy World

Once you've figured out your message and your audience, you can start working to align them. This is called finding your voice. Voice is one of those things that very few people understand.

Most people believe that finding your voice means creating content or experimenting with different ideas in general until the heavens open up and a booming voice says, "This is what you were born to do. This is your calling."

Umm … it doesn't work like that.

Instead, finding your voice is a process, the process of aligning your message and your audience.

If you want to find your voice, you need to find an audience, and test content until you figure out what your audience needs. You must be excited about your content.

The content you're creating is an extension of you. It's pushing forward your message—your mission—and, ideally, it's meeting the needs of your audience. Ideally, your audience is excited about your content and excited about your message. Truthfully, it's not enough to just have one or the other.

You can't have only a strong message or only a passionate audience. You need both. This is where a lot of people make the mistake of thinking, "I really love talking about this so I'm just going to keep creating content related to it and eventually the right people will find me! Right?!"

Or they think, "I love doing this so much that there must be people out there who will love it as much as I do! Right?!" Wrong.

When your content resonates with you only, it will never lead to anything more than a hobby. If you're goal is to have a new hobby—great! You've succeeded. But if your goal is to build a business, create a second stream of income, start a nonprofit, build a robust networking platform, get a promotion, or do anything that turns you into an owner, then your message must fulfill a need too.

By association, your content must fulfill a need. This means you need to passionately create content *while* measuring your content's popularity. Which articles or videos perform the best in terms of view, clicks, and comments? Which pieces of content get the noisiest response, good or bad? Which generate the most leads? These are the pieces of content (and the niche audiences) you want to focus on.

Finding a small niche that needs what you have to offer is critical to getting your content and related venture to take off. The only way to gain traction in any market is by identifying a very specific niche. Think of your niche as a tire spike. The denser the ground, the sharper the spike needed to dig into it. The ground is the market. If you want to penetrate the market, you need to sharpen your niche as much as possible. If your spike is too big and too dull, it won't be able to penetrate.

The fastest and most effective way to penetrate a market is to target a very small "sharp" niche first, and then grow outward. Consider the online news organization the *Huffington Post*, which posts articles about everything from lifestyle and entertainment, to politics, science, technology and more. The *Post* is similar to the *New York Times* now in terms of web traffic, driving over 80,000,000 visitors to their website each month.

However, when the organization started, the *Huffington Post* had a very small following. At the time, they only wrote articles about a very specific side of politics. They started with a very small niche (a small spike) and, as a result, gained immediate traction in the media market. This allowed them to grow rapidly in the years that followed.

Notes

1. HubSpot. 'Search engine optimization statistics'. https://www
   .hubspot.com/marketing-statistics

2. Saleh, K. 'How effective is inbound marketing – statistics and
   trends' [infographic]. *Invesp*. https://www.invespcro.com/blog/how-
   effective-is-inbound-marketing/

17 Why a Good Story Will Make You More Money Than a Great Product

The story is what's going to get people excited.

—Blake Mycoskie

Person-to-person connections are at the center of ownership. In fact, *network*, is literally one of the three ownership-based investments you've been encouraged to start making in previous chapters—the other two being knowledge and ability.

On the road to *Intelligent Achievement*, your pursuits will require you to deal with people.

One way or another, you need to know how to recruit help, and influence others in some way. You will surely be required to solve problems larger than yourself. This is where storytelling comes in.

Storytelling is an age-old concept that brings people together and keeps them engaged. People identify with stories. They also engage emotionally with stories. Scientific studies show that telling someone a story activates their entire brain, while telling them statistics and facts only activates quarter-size regions of their brain.[1]

This is why there is an entire field of psychology, called *narrative therapy*, devoted to changing people's lives through telling stories. When people read a story, they automatically step into the role of the story's protagonist.[2]

They see themselves as the hero and actively learn from whatever the hero does as if it's happening to them. They engage with content in a first-person way, and that makes storytelling a very powerful marketing strategy.

It doesn't matter where in the world you're based or how much money you may have, a good story will give a big voice to even the smallest venture. This is why you must invest time developing and mastering your approach to storytelling.

For the remainder of this chapter, we are going to discuss exactly how to create persuasive stories, how to add credibility to your storytelling, and how to mold your ideas into actionable takeaways.

How Storytelling Creates Influence and Ownership

Storytelling is also the most effective way to differentiate yourself from not only everyone in a particular market, but from everyone else in the world. A lot of entre-employees who first start creating content say things like, "There are just too many other financial traders in the world for me to be successful with this."

Or, "There are so many interior designers, I'll never make it!" Or, "How can I compete with millions of other single parents?!" If you're thinking like this, you're exactly right. Why would anyone read your content if it's just a collection of facts and how-to lists?

Creating content that just includes facts about your ideas is a recipe for failure. You'll never be able to write facts better than Wikipedia, or eHow, or a thousand other content websites that deal exclusively in dry information.

The only way to differentiate yourself is to tell your story. You, and you alone, own your story—and telling your story is the key to owning your audience's attention. No matter what you do, there are a lot of other people who work in your field, but there's only one you. There's only one person who's ever gone through your life story.

Whether you're writing a blog post or article, recording a video, or creating slides for a webinar or live seminar, start with a personal story that is relevant to the message of your content.

If you plan to build an online business that sells school supplies while simultaneously teaching parents how to buy the best supplies for their kids, start your next piece of content by telling a story about how you didn't have the right school supplies for your son. If you're an interior designer, tell the story about how you used to have a poorly designed apartment and how it negatively affected your personal life.

Be the hero of your story—but do it with humility.

The Hero's Story

Every story has a protagonist, a hero. In your stories, that hero is you, but you're not an arrogant hero. Instead, you're the humble warrior.

Realize that no one wants to read a story about perfection. No one cares about how great you are or how great you've always been. Instead, they want to hear about your problems. They want to know what you've overcome in the past and what you've learned in the process.

They want to identify with you. And, in reality, we're all deeply flawed heroes, aren't we?

The reason your readers and clients want to hear about your failures is so they can step into your shoes and learn from your mistakes. And that brings us to the next necessary storytelling element: your stories need to have an arc.

They need to describe, in detail, the problems you've faced and how you overcame them. This arc is often referred to as a monomyth or the Hero's Story.

Think of the last movie you watched. Who was the main character? What was their daily life like? Did they wake up every day and feel amazing until the book or movie ended? Did they wake up every day successful in every way until the credits started to roll?

Of course not! Instead, they had a series of problems and challenges at the beginning of the movie, worked to overcome them, had a climactic breakthrough, and then passed the lessons they learned onto others. This is, in essence, the Hero

Story and it's the story you need to use to communicate your ideas.

The Hero's Story starts with a hero who gets confronted with a challenge that they're not ready for in some way. Maybe they lack confidence, knowledge, or skills—either way, they wrestle with self-doubt and external ridicule. Most often, they shy away from taking on this challenge at first, but then life forces them to engage. Once they engage, they fail.

Then, they fail again … and again, and again, and again.

Here is where the arc starts. It is also the most critical part of the storytelling process.

By talking about the failures you've faced, you utilize the Hero's Story format to show your vulnerability and authenticity. Telling your story in this way draws in your readers emotionally and helps them identify with you.

As the Hero's Story continues, the hero learns from each failure and slowly starts to make progress. Eventually this cycle of failing and learning leads to a peak moment, or breakthrough. The hero succeeds, internally or externally, and then acts to pass along this success to others.

Only by willingly talking about your past mistakes and challenges will you put yourself in a credible position to talk about how you successfully overcame these obstacles. Your stories can include other people and other people's problems, and you can discuss your successes with confidence and charisma. You can have fun and be playful; but overall you want to be authentic, and you want to teach a lesson—the lesson that you learned the hard way.

Add Credibility and Practicality to Your Story

While discussing your past failures will give your story some
substance, you also need to prop it up with references. In other
words, you need to "give it legs."

The goal here is simply to build trust with those reading
your story by delivering some hard facts to back up what you're
saying. By referencing primary scientific research articles,
or other established sources such as the *New York Times* or
the *Harvard Business Review*, you can quickly add a layer of
credibility to your story.

The key here is to prove, to the best of your ability, that
the stance you're taking with your article is true. Let's say you
wrote that trading commodities is a mistake for middle-aged
homeowners.

Prove it. Explain why it's true. Give an example of
someone, somewhere, who had a bad experience trading
commodities in their 60s so the reader can see and hear your
points in action. Readers love images and story.

The goal is to build your case to the best of your ability.
The case you're making doesn't need to be airtight, but it does
need to be logical.

Once your story has legs, you need to make those legs
run. Make your story actionable. In general, people consume
content for three main reasons: to define *what* something is, to
understand *why* something is important, or to learn *how* to get
something done.

Either way, their goal is to gain actionable knowledge that
they can immediately apply to their life, thereby improving
their situation in some way. The best way to make your story
practical in this way is to distill your ideas down into very

actionable takeaways that directly answer the what, why, and how questions behind your ideas.

What are your ideas exactly? Why are they important? How can they be applied to everyday life? The best strategy for making your story actionable is to first break down the core message into a set number of points, and then back these points with strong opinions.

The worst thing you can do when trying to get your content read and shared is to sit on the fence with an idea. If you write to please everyone, you'll please no one. You've got to cut through the noise—and that's impossible to do without taking a side in your story. The only way to be heard is to draw a line in the sand and defend your side vigorously.

The most important part of taking a side is telling other people what they should do. Yes, you read that right.

Tell other people what to do. If you're writing a blog post or creating content to back up your business or venture, you're writing an opinion piece. So, give your opinion.

Give a command.

Your messaging can be polite or in line with whatever your personal brand may be, but don't fall into the trap of pleading your case through your content. If you don't believe in your message enough to recommend it strongly to others, why would anyone else believe in it? Why would they believe in you? Why would they trust you?

Choosing the Right Words

Now that you understand how to create content that resonates with both you and your audience, you need to learn how to make it meaningful to Google and other online search engines. In today's market, you can have the best content in the world, but if it doesn't rank well online, very few people will be able to find it, let alone read it. This is where adding the right words and phrases, or "keywords," to your content becomes essential.

Without understanding and using keywords correctly as part of your content marketing strategy, your venture will struggle to get attention. Keywords are important because they are what search engines use to identify and rank all online content.

For example, any time you go onto Google and search "how to … " or "what is … " the specific words you entered will be run through a series of complicated search algorithms and billions of indexed web pages to give you the most relevant content related to your search.

When you click on a page that comes up in a Google search, you instantly become part of that webpage's "organic web traffic."

As an entre-employee, your goal is to drive as much organic web traffic as possible to your website and overall venture. Organic traffic is the most valuable because it essentially lasts forever.

Once you create a piece of content online, it will remain on the internet forever, which means it will be indexed by Google forever (or as long as Google stays in business and the web exists, which looks like it will be a while).

Most importantly, as long as people keep navigating to your piece of content, Google will continue to rank it.

Over time, as more and more people navigate to it, the content will rank higher and higher.

The critical part of using keywords as part of your content marketing strategy is knowing which keywords to use. It doesn't matter if you rank high on Google for a particular keyword if that keyword has nothing to do with your goals. The keywords you embed in your content must target your niche audience.

The problem is it's impossible to know with 100% certainty which specific keywords your audience is using online.

You can use Google's Keyword Planner and other similar tools to get an idea of what they're searching for, but the only way to know for sure is to test your content consistently. As mentioned previously, you can do this by regularly publishing different blog articles and seeing which perform the best (get the most clicks, comments, shares).

Similarly, you can test smaller pieces of content on social media to see what gets you the most engagement. Over time, some pieces and social media posts will start to stand out. What keywords do these articles and posts have in common? What overall ideas and themes do they share? Dig through the content and find out.

Finally, pay close attention to the keywords that your audience uses when they comment on your articles and posts.

Imagine again that you sell school supplies online as part of your first entre-employee venture, and let's say you recently wrote an article about the five safest coloring markers for preschoolers. In the article, you use the phrases "coloring markers" and "magic markers" repeatedly. The article has performed well, and your audience is engaging with you.

Which phrase do you see used more in their comments, coloring markers or magic markers? Determine this, and you've determined one of the best keywords to use in your articles moving forward. What your audience says and writes is highly valuable, and staying in touch with them is essential to being a successful entre-employee.

Remember, ownership relies on attention and attention relies on your audience resonating with your message. What better way to align your audience with your message than to use their own words when communicating with them?

Notes

1. Haven, K. (2007) 'Story proof: The science behind the startling power of story'. https://www.amazon.com/Story-Proof-Science-Behind-Startling/dp/1591585465

2. Fields, D. (2010) 'Of two minds: Listener brain patterns mirror those of the speaker'. *Scientific American.* https://blogs.scientificamerican.com/guest-blog/of-two-minds-listener-brain-patterns-mirror-those-of-the-speaker/

18 The Magic of Turning Your Message into a Magnet

Not adding value is the same as taking it away.

—Seth Godin

Before the internet, bricks-and-mortar businesses stored all of their contacts in a company Rolodex, which was a desktop card index used to record names, addresses, and telephone numbers, in the form of a rotating spindle or a small tray to which removable cards were attached.

A company's Rolodex was its lifeblood and each employee's most valuable asset. If you had a robust enough Rolodex, no one would fire you. Even if you were fired, you'd be back on your feet in no time because of all your clients and connections. Today, the same is true of your email subscription list.

Google or Facebook can change their algorithm and limit the number of people you can access. LinkedIn can label you as a self-promoter and freeze your account. The bank can bankrupt you and seize your assets. Email service providers can even suspend you from their software programs. But no one can take away your connections.

That is, of course, as long as you have the contact information of your connections. The best way to protect yourself is to back up your email lists consistently.

As long as you have an Excel or another spreadsheet file of your most up-to-date email lists in hand, you are in control of your fate. When it comes to your email lists, back them up regularly and store hard copies.

More than anything else, the size and strength of your virtual Rolodex, which is to say the size and strength of your email list, or *network*, will determine the success of any venture you take on.

Lead Magnets Create Two-Way Value

The most important part of building up a strong virtual Rolodex is collecting other people's contact information and giving value to them in return. These two processes can be done simultaneously by creating a lead magnet.

A lead magnet is simply an informational resource, such as a how-to guide, a tip sheet, a free video series, a white paper, or an eBook that's offered to your target audience to determine their interest in a future product or service.

In this way, lead magnets create two-way value. When it comes to generating leads for an active sales funnel, which we will discuss in later chapters, a lead magnet is a free, information-based gift that sits at the beginning of the funnel to bring in leads. Very often, lead magnets are loss leaders, which are products given away or sold at a loss to attract customers.

The good news is that if you're creating content consistently, you already have everything you need to create a strong lead magnet.

While there are many types of lead magnets, eBooks are the simplest and most effective magnets to create using the content we've discussed in previous chapters. Creating an eBook is simple because you only need a handful of blog articles to create your first eBook.

By blogging and using your writing to create an eBook, you're killing many birds with a single stone. First, you're adding written content to your venture's website, which is the best way to increase your ranking on Google and other search engines.

Second, you're giving your readers and clients consistent value for free. Third, you're staying in touch with your readers through your content, testing your ideas as well as their needs continuously. Fourth and finally, you're building up a library of content that you can repackage for future initiatives down the road, such as informational products, sales pages, and more.

The first step to creating an eBook is to evaluate which articles people have been reading the most. The best way to evaluate this is with a free third-party tracking software such as Google Analytics or a *most popular* box plugin, both of which can be integrated into any current website platform, such as WordPress, SquareSpace, or Weebly.

Many current websites will automatically tell you which pages are being viewed the most.

This *unique views* metric is all you need to determine how your articles rank in popularity. Once you know the ranking of your blog articles, you can select the top five or so articles you've posted and rework them into an eBook. Here, the key is to fit the pieces under a unified theme.

For example, if you write reviews for different types of products for women. First, ask yourself, "What do all of these products have in common?" If the answer is that all the products are aimed at successful women in leadership positions, then your eBook might be called *Living the Lifestyle of a Successful Woman*.

If, on the other hand, you write about women who work in corporate careers and your most successful articles are on the topic of how successful women balance their home life with their work life, then your eBook might be called *Corporate Success and Balance for Women*.

How to Create an EBook Lead Magnet

When it comes to driving people to take action to download it, the most important parts of any eBook are the title and the cover image. Period.

This is particularly the case when you're creating an eBook that you will offer for "free" online in exchange for a reader's contact information.

The only part of the eBook itself that people will likely be able to see before they decide whether or not to download it is the title and cover. When creating your eBook's title, there are two questions you must answer: "Who is this for?" and "What is the result?"

First, make sure your eBook calls attention to the identity of your target audience as directly as possible. If your audience consists of homeowners who make more than $100,000 a year, call your eBook *The $100K+ Homeowners Guide to XYZ*. The key here is to be specific. Remember, the smaller niche always wins.

Name your eBook in a way that identifies the smallest, most engaged niche. Second, provide a clear result in the title. What result does your eBook provide? What problem is it solving?

If your audience loves articles about traveling in Europe, and your eBook is about traveling in France, then write this result directly in the title of the eBook: *100K+ Homeowners Guide to Traveling France*. Do not use, *100K+ Homeowners Guide to Traveling Europe* or worse, *100K+ Homeowners Guide to Traveling Abroad*.

For the eBook's cover, you should use bright colors that assertively grab other people's attention. Imagine someone scrolling through their Facebook feed rapidly, skimming it at light speed—this is your audience. Bright orange, red, blue, green, and yellow colors are best for this.

You should also use a representative image to capture the attention (and intrigue) of potential subscribers.

Imagery is the one part of content creation where it pays to be symbolic. For example, if your eBook is in fact titled *100K+ Homeowners Guide to Traveling France*, the cover should not merely show a picture of France or the picture of a homeowner (or worse, the picture of a homeowner somewhere in France). Here, readers will be less likely to download your eBook because there's no intrigue—no mystery, interest, or more practically, no reason to click. Instead, the cover should show two wine glasses and a half-eaten croissant.

If you show a suitcase packed with white sand, or a luxurious hotel towel, you will create more intrigue. You will create a small paradox in your reader's mind, one that can only be resolved by downloading the eBook. Use images and designs that create subconscious intrigue.

For your eBook's title, be concise and clear. *Never sacrifice clarity to cleverness here.*

Once you have a few title and cover ideas, you should A/B test them using online polls, social media, email surveys, or simply by asking friends and family. With a sound title and cover in place, you can compile your eBook as a simple, downloadable PDF (portable document format).

When finalizing the body of your eBook, be sure to include the best content from your most popular blog articles, as discussed above. However, do not make the mistake of merely throwing the content together into the eBook as-is.

Instead, go back through your selected items and adapt the content as needed. Update titles and subtitles. Rearrange the order of the main sections, delete inappropriate or irrelevant links, update references, and write transition sentences between paragraphs and between articles to ensure the eBook flows from chapter to chapter.

Overall, you want the quality of your eBook to be high enough to attract subscribers for at least 6 to 12 months before you have to update it.

Finally, if you have been creating video blogs instead of blog articles, you can still create an eBook by recording a video for each chapter instead of writing each chapter. Here, you will be delivering a short video series to subscribers.

The process of delivering your eBook or eBook video series to a reader who subscribes, as well as collecting their email address in exchange for the lead magnet, is covered in the following chapters.

Lead magnets not only create two-way value, they create two-way ownership. By crafting something your audience can download and literally own, you will establish even more trust with them. This trust will once again be reciprocated with your audience, further releasing the reins on their attention. They will more quickly and easily give you their attention, which will in turn elevate you as an owner.

19 How to Build up Your Virtual Rolodex

The most important things in life are the connections you make with others.

—Tom Ford

Any point of contact between you and a potential client is known as a *touch point*. To make a sale, you'll need to contact your readers and potential customers at least seven times.

The fastest and most effective way to collect these touch points is with email marketing, or similar mass communication means such as Facebook Messenger or mobile phone messaging. But before you can market by email, you have to build up your email list, or virtual Rolodex.

The only way to make your virtual Rolodex grow is to capture leads, and the best way to capture leads is with lead capture boxes and pages, collectively referred to as lead capture "forms."

There are several types of lead capture forms, but the most critical to converting web traffic into email subscribers are feature boxes, splash pages, and squeeze pages.

A squeeze page (also referred to as a landing page) is simply a web page created solely to solicit opt-in email addresses from prospective subscribers. It's called a squeeze page because the page only offers the visitor one of two options, to enter their contact information or to close the page.

In other words, the visitor is *squeezed* into subscribing. For this reason, you want to make sure that you do not add any extra links on your squeeze pages.

Squeeze and Splash Your Followers

Creating an active squeeze page is a very effective way to capture other people's contact information. As we discussed, this is most often done by offering a lead magnet, such as an eBook or video series, in exchange for the other person's email address.

All a squeeze page needs to be effective is a *call to action*, a well-designed graphic of what you're offering, information describing the *result* that your offering provides, an email subscription box, and a subscribe button. You do not need to be a web developer to create squeeze page. In fact, you don't even need a website to have a squeeze page. Instead, you can use a landing page service provider such as Lead Pages[1] or ClickFunnels[2] to quickly generate a variety of squeeze pages and start collecting email addresses right away.

A splash page, on the other hand, is simply a page on top of your landing page or website that a visitor sees first before being given the option to continue to the main content of the site.

Splash pages can come in the form of smaller pop-up windows, or they can be full web pages that appear in front of other pages.

If you're a rational living person, you're probably thinking, "I hate pop-up windows!"

Sure, everyone hates those old annoying spam windows that used to pop up on your 1998 web browser and never go away. But, nowadays, splash pages are much more elegant. More importantly, today's splash pages have a data-driven purpose.

There are several website plugins that allow you to create artistic and informative splash pages that can link to a squeeze page with a lead magnet or directly to a lead magnet itself.

Annoying or not, research on website user activity shows that people are more likely to enter their contact information somewhere on a website *after* viewing a splash page, even if they initially closed the splash page. That's right, your readers might be annoyed by the splash, but they're more likely to give you their contact information after seeing it.

What is a CTA Feature Box?

A CTA feature box is a boxed portion of a web page that actively encourages visitors to sign up to an email subscription list. Most commonly, this feature box sits at the top of a website's homepage. However, feature boxes can be used anywhere on any content page.

For example, you can put a feature box at the end of a blog article, next to a video window, or on a squeeze page or splash page.

The only requirement for a CTA feature box is a strong call to action, which usually involves a lead magnet offer and an opt-in email form. An opt-in email form is simply a text box that prompts people to enter their name and email address. Of course, every feature box also contains a subscriber button of some kind that, when pressed, initiates an automated email subscription process and delivers the lead magnet to the email of the person who subscribed.

The most important part of a CTA feature box is its call to action, or call to actions.

A call to action, or CTA, is a clear instruction to an audience to provoke an immediate response, usually using an imperative verb such as "*Sign up* now," "*Learn* more," or "*Get the free eBook*."

A strong CTA has three parts: a target audience, a results-oriented offer, and an instruction. For example, "Sign up below to get my free *Interior Design For Men* eBook and start entertaining powerful and attractive guests" is a strong CTA because it targets a specific audience (men), offers something specific (eBook on interior design that will show you how to entertain more people), and provides a clear instruction (sign up below).

Other CTAs, such as those embedded in your email subscription buttons, can be shorter: "Subscribe now" or "Click to
download."

The best way to craft a quality CTA feature box is to
carefully consider both the audience you are targeting and the
message of the box itself.

Recall that these two things—message and audience—are
critical to giving your content a voice. The more specific and
result-oriented the message, and the more targeted audience,
the more likely you are to capture someone's contact information, and the more likely you are to capture the *right* person's
contact information.

Remember, your goal here is to own your network, or at
least your network's contact information. This means you must
not only keep your virtual Rolodex up to date, and back it up
consistently, but you must also aggressively grow the size of
your network using the lead capture forms described above.
Once you have one or several CTA feature boxes in place,
and one or many squeeze and splash pages created, it's time to
connect these lead capture forms to an email service provider.

Case Study #3: Tim Bushnell, PhD

"Comic Sans is the worst font. I quit."

Tim Bushnell is the director of all the core research facilities at the University of Rochester Medical Center, which is
one of the top medical centers in the world.

Tim loves his job, but he always had a desire to do more.
He didn't like the feeling of being dependent on only one

paycheck or being confined to only one career, so Tim started experimenting with some other pursuits.

First, Tim began writing blog articles on various scientific topics and publishing these articles on other people's websites. This satisfied some of his creative desires, but it wasn't exactly lucrative.

Next, Tim started doing some side work for a training company that specialized in flow cytometry, a scientific technique that was gaining in popularity and was being used for all types of research, cancer or otherwise. Tim had worked in the field of flow cytometry for nearly 10 years, so the side job seemed like a good fit. He would teach, write course materials, create other training content for the company, and get paid for it.

The new job satisfied Tim for a couple of years, but then things took a turn for the worse. The owners of the company became obsessed with small things, like using Comic Sans for all PowerPoint slide presentations.

"If the text isn't in Comic Sans, you can't show it to our clients!" they'd say to Tim.

"How did I get here?" Tim thought.

Somehow, he now had two bosses. The University of Rochester and now this flow cytometry training company too. That's when Tim decided to quit. Two years later, due to poor management, the training company ended up going out of business.

After some reflection, Tim decided to become an owner; he decided to start his own flow cytometry training company, Expert Cytometry.

At first, Expert Cytometry was nothing more than a blog. Tim wrote articles on the latest developments in the field of flow cytometry. Then, he started to use the content to market his teaching services. Content marketing became Tim's second job. He reworked and repackaged a handful of his articles to create a downloadable ebook, *Modern Flow Cytometry*, which he offered online to his readers.

Over time, Tim's virtual Rolodex of email subscribers built up to over 20,000 scientists. Tim went on to develop a minimum viable product that was more scalable than his teaching and consulting services: the Flow Cytometry Mastery Class.

Expert Cytometry is now the world's largest independent flow cytometry training platform, and the Mastery Class has over 1,000 paying members who renew annually. Meanwhile, Tim's ebook, *Modern Flow Cytometry*, has been downloaded more than 100,000 times.

Tim still works at the University of Rochester and considers himself an entre-employee who finally got the "entre" part right.

Notes

1. LeadPages. 'Start with high-performing templates, then make them yours'. https://www.leadpages.net
2. ClickFunnels. https://www.clickfunnels.com

20 Developing and Automating a Message-Driven Content

Communication—the human connection—is the key to personal and career success.

—Paul J. Meyer

Regardless of which venture you are pursuing on your way to ultimate levels of ownership, the email list associated with that venture is your virtual Rolodex. Without a viable email list, that venture does not exist.

When it comes to ownership, your virtual Rolodex is your most valuable asset. To fully understand the value of an email list, you must understand what an email list is and how it can be leveraged to generate value.

An electronic mailing subscription list, or email list, is a specific way of using emails to distribute information to many internet users. These email lists are similar to a traditional mailing list (a collection of names and physical mailing addresses) that organizations have used for decades to send out physical items such as magazines or jars of jelly to their readers, members, and customers.

In general, an email list requires four things: a list of email addresses, the people ("subscribers") receiving mail at those addresses, the content (email messages) sent to those addresses, and a *reflector*, which is a single email address that, when designated as the recipient of a message, will send a copy of that message to all of the subscribers.

Connecting a lead capture form (see the previous chapter) to an email list allows you to store an email subscriber's contact information automatically. You can also use it to access this subscriber's contact information and send them information (via an email) at will.

To create an email list, all you need is a piece of paper and a pen. However, while pen and paper might be a handy way to collect the contact details of a small live audience at a local workshop, it's not an effective or sustainable way to collect hundreds of email addresses entered online daily from all around the world. For this, you need an email service provider, such as Mail Chimp, Infusionsoft, or AWeber.

There are dozens of email service providers to choose from and most allow you to try their service for free up to a certain number of email subscriptions, and most provide easy-to-follow instructions for connecting your lead capture forms to their service.

The main advantage of using an email service provider is that you can automatically collect and store hundreds, or even hundreds of thousands, of people's contact details and recall these details as needed.

How to Leverage an Email Subscription List

Once you've linked your lead capture forms to an email service, all your subscribers' contact information will be automatically stored in the email list you created. Over time, you can segment your lists based on your subscribers' individual interests. For example, people who are interested in fishing in Canada (based on the fact that they downloaded your free Canadian fishing guide) could be put on one list titled "Canadian Fishers," while people who are interested in fishing in America (based on the fact they downloaded your free American fishing guide) could be put on a second list titled "American Fishers."

The key is that each list is connected to at least one lead capture form. You can segment your subscribers based on their interests, locations, gender, age, income level, email activity level, and a variety of other characteristics.

With your lists in place, you can now start sending your first email marketing campaigns. Email marketing refers to directly marketing a commercial message to a group of people using email. In its broadest sense, every email sent to any email subscriber on your email list could be considered email marketing.

An email marketing *campaign* is simply a way to describe sending an email or series of emails strategically to certain subscribers or all subscribers on your email list. The very first email marketing campaign every person, business, or venture should set up is a Real Simple Syndication (RSS) campaign, which allows you to automatically deliver content such as blog articles or video blogs to your email subscribers.

RSS campaigns use special bits of information to pull in content from your blog every time you add new content. When you post a new article, your email service provider will pull this content from your website into the campaign and send it to your subscribers on a daily, weekly, or monthly schedule.

An RSS campaign is also known as an RSS feed and can be referred to as a *drip campaign* or an *autoresponder*. Either way, the concept is the same: your subscribers are sent marketing emails automatically on a schedule.

You can also create one-time email campaigns by manually adding content to an email and sending it to subscribers on your email list. For example, if you wanted to send your subscribers a survey to gain feedback on their needs, you could draft an email and schedule it to be sent only once, rather than on a recurring basis.

Why Email Marketing Will Always be Valuable

Email has been around for more than 20 years,[1] which makes it a dinosaur in the technology world. However, no matter how many innovations come out, it's still one of the best marketing tools out there.

In fact, it's become more effective in recent years. That's because new tools allow you to automate your email process, personalize mass emails, and even measure the email campaign's effectiveness.

Email marketing will continue to be valuable, even with the rise of text message marketing, because people are used to subscribing to other people's ventures in this way.

They are not, on the other hand, used to subscribing by entering their phone number and responding to automated text messages. Sure, this may change in the future, but what will not change is the fact that telecom companies are ahead of the curve in combating SMS marketing, text message marketing, and mass texting.

Here's the difference: email marketing developed long before anyone had a strategy in place for fighting against email spam. In fact, email marketing developed long before anyone knew exactly what email spam was or how to identify it.

As a result, all battles to fight against email marketing are uphill battles. SMS marketing, text message marketing, and mass texting, on the other hand, developed after the idea of online spam was deeply ingrained into everyone's psyche.

More importantly, it developed after people and companies created very effective anti-spam strategies and after governments started passing more stringent anti-spam laws.

Email marketing is here to stay—and not just because it developed before other forms of online marketing, but because it's a very easy way to interact with subscribers directly.

Email Marketing and the Last Gatekeepers

Like other forms of *direct* content marketing, email marketing allows you to communicate directly and personally with individuals, rather than through so-called key opinion leaders, media elite, big retailers, or gatekeepers of any kind.

As a result, subscribers are much more likely to develop a personal relationship with you and your venture, which makes them much more likely to spread your message, rally to your cause, and buy your products and services.

For example, online analytical studies show that conversion rates, in terms of sales per email subscriber on an email list, average 7% when a sale is promoted by email marketing.[2] Conversely, these conversion rates drop to 1% when any other form of online marketing is used, including social media marketing and affiliate marketing.

Email marketing is how all of your content marketing efforts will finally become actualized.

First, readers (or *users*) will visit your website and lead capture pages. These visitors are referred to as your website traffic or simply your *traffic*. A certain number of these visitors will subscribe to your lead capture forms to receive one or more of your lead magnets.

Once they subscribe, they will be automatically added to your email list and will automatically start to receive any of your automated email campaigns, such as an RSS campaign.

Now, you have the chance to build trust with your subscriber (and potentially turn your subscriber into a paying client).

By delivering emails that either contain valuable content or are linked to valuable content, and by delivering these emails consistently, you will start to build both trust and loyalty with your subscribers.

Over time, your subscribers will come to expect your free content. They will also start to engage with it, commenting on it, sharing it, and moving on to other content you have to offer through embedded links and your website in general.

The final step of the content marketing process involves you and your venture offering a paid-for product or service to your subscribers, thereby moving them through a sales funnel, while also working to turn these new paying clients into lifetime clients by moving them through a larger product funnel.

The most important thing to remember during your email marketing efforts is that *every piece of content you deliver is leading to the sale of something.* Unless your venture is a hobby, it will need to turn a profit. Even nonprofit ventures need to bring in money in the form of donations. As such, you must learn to structure your content and the delivery of your content with this in mind.

Don't forget the *marketing* in content marketing.

Remember, the key to ownership here is to market a message, and eventually a product that fulfills a need. The only way to do this effectively is to strategically map out when and how you will be "launching" your messages, and products or services, as well as how you will communicate these launches to your email subscribers. The remainder of this section will focus on these topics.

Notes

1. Gateway Commercial Finance. '5 Reasons why you can't ignore email marketing'. https://gatewaycfs.com/bff/ob/5-reasons-why-you-can't-ignore-email-marketing

2. Kissmetrics. 'Email crushes social media'. Kissmetrics Blog. https://blog.kissmetrics.com/email-crushes-social-media/

21 Turning Your Message into a Minimum Viable Product

I do not think there is any thrill that can go through the human heart like that felt by the inventor as he sees some creation of the brain unfolding to success ... Such emotions make a man forget food, sleep, friends, love, everything.

—Nikola Tesla

The road to ownership is paved with *your* knowledge, network, and ability.

We have discussed the link between content marketing and investing in your *network* in detail.

But what about *knowledge* and *ability*?

If you've been paying attention to the in-depth information presented in the last several chapters, you've likely already expanded your knowledgebase in the field of content marketing extensively. You may have noticed that you're slowly but surely learning an entirely new skill set—a set of new, professional abilities.

In the same way, your progress on the path to creative ownership and *Intelligent Achievement* overall relies on the continual uptake of new, useful information that can be applied to a productive end.

Here, the productive end is *a product that solves a problem.*

What is a Minimum Viable Product?

Now that you've analyzed your message-driven content and identified what your potential clients need, you're ready to start turning your message into a product. The problem is that developing a product of any kind is risky. Product development takes extensive time, energy, and resources.

The risk is that you will invest heavily in a product that will end up performing poorly in the marketplace.

The only way to curb this risk is to develop what is called a *minimum viable product*, or *MVP*.

MVPs have a high return on investment versus risk because instead of investing everything in the product and then testing it in the market, you've invested just enough—the absolute "minimum"—to make the product "viable" in the market. In other words, you've made the product just functional enough to survive testing.

MVPs can come in the form of informational goods and services such as video training programs, live webinar courses, audio podcasts, consulting calls, and typed documentation;

or it can come in the form of physical goods and services like wristbands, shoes, furniture, hairstyling, massage therapy, and more.

Here, we will focus on informational products and services that can be sold and delivered online without physical shipping. We will concentrate on this model because it provides the fastest and most effective way for entre-employees to create a second stream of income without disrupting their current professional situation.

A successful product is a result of massive need. The more your readers, users, followers, and fans need your product, the more likely they are to buy it. The problem is it can be tough to determine what your potential customers need.

This is why so many lifestyle businesses create products that fail in the marketplace.

The owners of these businesses forget to test product need.

Instead, they just start building the products that they're excited about. Recall that finding your voice requires aligning your message with your audience's needs. Similarly, creating a successful product requires aligning a message with your potential clients' needs.

The fastest and most effective way to determine what your potential clients need is to, first, determine the content they're engaging with the most and, second, build an MVP around the message of this content.

Remember that testing content is the best way to determine what your readers, users, followers, and fans need. By developing an MVP around your most popular content, you can reduce the risk of creating a product nobody wants.

You also ensure that the product you develop is in line with your message.

Don't make the mistake of creating an MVP based on someone else's content or someone else's opinion.

When you do this, you create a product that's in line with another person's message and another person's platform, not your own. You also run the risk of creating a product that you will eventually lose interest in because it's not built around your message.

Remember the "M" in MVP

Moving from finding a message to creating an MVP is where a lot of entre-employees get stuck. These entre-employees think they need to build the perfect product before they can sell it. They see product development as a monumental task. In short, they forget the "M" or the "minimum" in MVP.

The truth is, creating an MVP can be as simple as putting ten blog articles together into an eBook that you sell, or hosting three webinars and then putting those webinars together into a video training package. When it comes to creating an MVP, don't overthink it.

Instead, create the simplest product possible that will help your potential clients in some way, and start selling it.

Once your MVP is on the market, you'll learn very quickly what your potential customers are willing to buy as well as what they like (or don't like) about your product once they buy it.

The good news is that, even if no one buys your product at first, you'll have invested very little into it, which means you can quickly and easily tweak it into something better, or create an entirely new product altogether.

Best of all, since you've followed the sequence of crafting your message first, then building your platform, then creating your product, you'll still have your message and platform in place. The only thing you'll have to do is launch another product.

If you still find yourself forgetting the "M" in your MVP, remember this: your product doesn't matter. Let that sink in. The reason your product doesn't matter is that people don't buy products anymore; they buy the marketing in front of products.

When it comes to developing your MVP, the most important thing to realize is that people will rarely buy your product for the product itself. Instead, they will buy what your marketing tells them about your product.

They will buy what other people are saying about your product or the social proof of your product.

They will buy you and your brand.

What matters are you, your message, your brand, your marketing, and your ongoing relationship with your potential clients.

As soon as you get a reasonable amount of content created—whether it's in the form of blog articles, videos, webinars, podcasts, or anything else—you should start organizing and collating your content into an MVP.

For example, you could collect 20–30 of your top blog articles and repackage them into four modular workbooks. You could then record four 30-minute video presentations based on these workbooks and load all of this content onto a password protected web page. *Voilà!*—You're done.

Seriously, this is all your need for your MVP!

Whether or not your MVP will sell depends entirely on your marketing materials, such as your sales emails and sales pages. Your success will also rely on the size and engagement of your email subscriber list.

Perfection is the enemy of an MVP!

Yes, you should work hard to create a high-quality MVP that has the power to help as many of your potential customers as possible. However, you should also realize that the best way to determine what will help your potential clients is to develop an MVP as quickly as possible and start getting feedback right away.

The faster you get feedback, the faster you can improve your MVP.

Over time, your MVP will turn into a flagship product—an exceptional offering tied strongly to your message and brand that perfectly solves your customers' problems.

Growing an MVP into a Flagship Product

Every MVP should be created with the intention of turning it into a flagship product.

To develop your MVP into a flagship product, you must continue to test and tweak your MVP to near perfection.

This means you must adopt a researcher's mindset and start collecting as much feedback on your MVP as possible, as soon as it enters the market.

As mentioned, the fastest and most effective way to gather feedback on your MVP is through your content marketing efforts.

However, your feedback efforts should not stop there. Instead, you should send out surveys to email subscribers using online survey platforms such as SurveyMonkey,[1] and you should leverage social media platform functionality such as Facebook polls.

You should also be engaging with your potential customers on an individual basis through email, Skype and phone calls, social media comments, social media private messages, and more.

The key to transforming an MVP into a flagship product is learning to appreciate criticism. The more critical your readers, users, followers, and fans are about your MVP, the better. Responding positively and productively to critical feedback is what will turn your MVP into a sensational flagship product and a steady, second stream of income. It is also what will turn you officially into an entre-employee and an owner. Now you've truly created something of real value—something you own that solves a problem and makes the world a better place. All that's left to do is introduce your creation to the world.

Note

1. Survey Monkey: Make better decisions with the world's number one survey platform. https://www.surveymonkey.com

22 What Happens When Your MVP Meets Your Market?

The world has changed, and the only true security is your ability to create value and get paid for that value.

—Jeff Walker

Once you've developed your MVP, you need to market it, sell it, and deliver it to your potential customers. The process of bringing your MVP to your market is referred to as launching your product.

A "product launch" is a marketing strategy consisting of a carefully planned and scheduled sequence of events with the initial goal of attracting as much attention as possible to the release of your MVP and the overall aim of converting as many sales of your MVP as possible.

The first step is to schedule the launch for a specific date and time. With the launch date in place, you can start alerting your email subscribers to the upcoming release of your product through various content marketing activities. This is known as the *prelaunch* phase. The prelaunch phase is critical, not only to converting sales on the first few days of your launch, but converting a high percentage of sales overall.

Once the prelaunch phase is over, you'll execute the *launch* phase. The launch phase includes a series of tightly executed touchpoints with your potential clients.

These touchpoints will occur in the form of a series of product launch emails that link your potential customers to your *product sales page*, which is simply a web page where your product is described in detail and available for purchase.

The Prelaunch Phase of a Product Launch

When it comes to launching an online product, the biggest mistake new entre-employees make is assuming their readers, users, followers, and fans are magically aware of their product's existence or their plans to launch a product. In reality, no one but you will be aware of your product launch until you start telling other people.

Even then, other people will need to be repeatedly notified of your upcoming product launch before it will enter into their conscious awareness. It's up to you to make your potential customers aware of your product.

The best way to do this during the prelaunch phase is to send a short email one to two months before your launch, alerting people to the fact that you have something special for them in development. At this point, you don't need to say anything more.

After you've alerted your potential customers that you're developing something exciting for them and their needs, you need to explain to them what your product is, how it's going to help them, and when you're going to make it available.

These three things should be laid out in a second short email sent to your potential customers two weeks before your launch, during the prelaunch phase. A similar email should also be sent one week before your launch and, again, the Friday before your launch. In your "Friday before" email, you will send one final email alerting your potential customers to the opening of your product's *salescart*, which is simply a page that allows someone to enter their credit card or other financial details and execute a *transaction* for your product.

This "Friday before" email is your final pre-launch email, and should be no more than three to five sentences. It should also contain a compelling call to action that instructs the reader to check their email inbox first thing Monday morning for the first "Open Cart" email.

It's crucial during the pre-launch phase that you make every effort to articulate the exclusivity of your product. Your product should only be available for three to ten days. After the final day, your sales page and salescart should be shut down.

Here, we will focus on the details of executing a five-day online product launch. Contrary to popular belief, no matter what your product is, or which market you're targeting, you will convert more sales during strategic three- to ten-day product launch periods than you will by keeping your product available for purchase year round. In addition, limiting your sales periods will free up your time to take better care of your customers during the rest of the year.

The Launch Phase of a Product Launch

The first day of the launch phase of your product launch should always start early in the week. For a five-day product launch, the first day should be early Monday morning. If you've followed the previous chapters closely and built an engaged platform, and if you've executed your pre-launch emails correctly, you should expect between 10 and 40% of your total launch sales to come in on this first day.

If you're on the lower end, don't stress. It's very common to receive over 50% of your sales on the last day of a five-day launch. That being said, you still need to execute the previous four days of the launch correctly in order to convert all of your expected last-day sales.

In terms of the content that you should include in your five-day product launch emails: on Monday, your messaging should be short and to the point. Your goal is merely to tell your potential clients that your product is available (the salescart is open), explain the key benefits of your product, and then provide a strong call to action to visit your sales page. On Tuesday, the second day of your launch, your goal is to show social proof. Who has purchased your product in the past?

Who recently purchased your product? What do these people have to say about it? The entire goal of your second email is to show your potential clients as many written and video testimonials as possible.

Your goal is to show people that they are one day late to the party. On Wednesday, the third day of the launch, you want to address any pain points your potential clients have.

What are their biggest needs? If you've executed your content marketing and product development strategies correctly, you'll know exactly what your clients' needs are. Now, it's time to highlight those needs by telling a story of someone who failed to buy your product, failed to meet their needs and, as a result, experienced a lot of pain.

Of course, this story must be true, and it should speak directly to those readers who suffer from analysis paralysis. You must make it clear that they need to make a decision to solve their problem and relieve their pain and, by not making a decision, they are deciding to stay in pain.

On Thursday, you'll want to do the opposite—you'll want to spotlight a product success story. In this fourth email, you'll want to call attention to one or two people who have used your product and achieved a positive result because of it, including the relief of whatever pain or discomfort they were experiencing before buying your product.

The last day of a product launch is by far the most important. This is because the sense of urgency your potential clients will feel is the highest. They must make a decision to get your product today and fix their problem, or "lose" your product and "lose" their chance to fix their problem.

On average, days two through four of a five-day launch will bring in only 10–20% of your product launch's total sales. However, as mentioned, day five will often bring in over 50% of your sales.

For this reason, the emails you send on day five should be hard-hitting and laced with urgency. You must communicate as directly as possible that today is the last day for people to buy your product and if they fail to buy, their current problem will continue, as will their pain.

This is best done by sending a series of short, punchy emails throughout the day. Don't make the mistake of being indirect. Do not make the mistake of tip toeing around your message. If you're doing it right, then you've created an MVP that is tailor-made to solve a very specific problem for a market you know intimately well. You truly believe in it. You know it will help people. Act like it.

This sales page, whether it's on your site or a simple squeeze page on any landing page software application, will be connected to a salescart managed by PayPal or some other third-party online payment system.

From here, all that's left to do is to deliver your product to your paying customers.

The fulfillment process is the third and final component of the product launch cycle.

Fulfillment, which is short for "order fulfillment," is simply the process of delivering your online product to your customers.

How to Fulfill an Online Product

This entire process, from product marketing up to product fulfillment, has been covered in the previous chapters.

First, you learned how to market your product through content marketing. Next, you learned how to recruit email subscribers through your blog articles and other free content, as well as through eBooks and other lead magnets.

Then, you learned how to develop an MVP and how to launch your MVP to your market. In the next chapter, you'll learn how to create a sales page that converts sales and turns your potential customers into paying customers. However, before you start selling your product, you need to have a plan for delivering your product to your clients once they've paid for it.

Once you've sold your product, you need to deliver it. In other words, once you've taken an order, you need to fulfill your order. If the product you're selling online is purely information, the fulfillment process is simple and can be set up by you alone.

If, however, you're selling a physical product, the fulfillment process is more complicated. In this latter case, you'll have to consider manufacturing methods and costs, as well as shipping methods and costs. Here, we will focus on informational products and services that can be fulfilled entirely online via email, websites, and other virtual means.

It's important to realize that the purpose of every product launch email you send is to drive your email subscribers to your sales page where they can purchase your product through a salescart, which is often nothing more than a payment page that's hosted by a third party online payment system such as PayPal, allowing you to add "buy buttons" to your sales pages that link directly to PayPal's readymade salescarts.

The key here is that once a customer purchases your product via PayPal, you will need to deliver your product to them. The fastest and most effective way to do this is to connect PayPal to your email service provider, such as Mail Chimp, Infusionsoft, or Aweber.

Once PayPal is connected to your email service provider, PayPal can feed your provider the name and email address of anyone who purchases your product.

You will want these names and email addresses delivered to a specified email list, and you will want this email list connected to an automated email campaign. Then, as soon as a new contact gets entered into the email list, the email campaign—in this case the *fulfillment email campaign*—is triggered and sent to the new contact.

The fulfillment campaign can simply include a "welcome email" with links to your informational product, or it can include a series of emails that are delivered weekly, parsing out the delivery of your informational product.

By mapping out a series of premeditated fulfillment emails, you can ensure your customers receive your product promptly while also ensuring they enjoy a pleasant experience after purchasing. Once again, you are protecting your clients' mental energy, setting them up to release more of their attention to you. On a long enough timeline, clients who are shown this kind of reverence for their attention turn into lifetime clients.

23 The Addiction of Vanity Analytics and How to Really Use Social Media

Vanity and pride are different things, though the words are often used synonymously. A person may be proud without being vain. Pride relates more to our opinion of ourselves, vanity to what we would have others think of us.

—Jane Austen

Social media marketing is *not* creative ownership.

Content marketing in general is only ownership when you control your own access to the knowledgebase, network, and/or special abilities associated with the content.

No matter how many Facebook or Twitter followers you have, they will never be *your* followers. They will only ever be Facebook and Twitter's followers. If either platform decided to delete your account, your followers disappear. This is not ownership.

Social media is also *not* an effective way to sell your online products.

You read that right.

In today's world, people do not go onto social media platforms to buy. They go onto social media platforms to be—you guessed it—social. You and everyone else in the world log into Facebook and Instagram, not to make a monetary transaction, but to make a social transaction. We use social media platforms to learn and share, not buy and trade.

As mentioned previously, online analytical studies show that conversion rates for selling through social media marketing are below 1%.[1] The same holds true for conversion rates for selling through affiliate marketing and multi-level marketing.

As a comparison, conversion rates for selling through email marketing are 7% and above. For this reason, your social media activities should focus primarily on increasing brand awareness and turning your readers, users, followers, and fans into email subscribers. By working to convert your social media followers into email subscribers, you are investing in your highest yield activity—the one that gives you 7% return versus a 1% or less return.

Social Media is a Means of Brand Awareness and Brand Protection Only

Brand awareness is simply the extent to which your customers and potential customers are familiar with the distinctive qualities or image of your product and overall business.

Brand awareness is a particularly important way of promoting online informational products. When it comes to informational products sold online, there are very few factors that differentiate a product from its competitors. As a result, the product that maintains the highest brand awareness compared to its competitors will get the most sales.

For example, there are several online training programs claiming to help people promote their products more effectively on Facebook.

However, very little separates these online training programs in terms of methodology. Facebook dictates how Facebook advertising works and each of these programs will simply explain this same process in slightly different ways.

That being said, customers who buy these online programs are very aware of brands like Gary Vaynerchuck and Amy Porterfield (even though you may not be). The reason these brands have more brand awareness is that these entre-employees strategically developed very strong product brands backed by even stronger personal brands. They've also worked hard to protect their brands.

If you want to be a successful entre-employee for more than a few days, you will need to do the same.

The Big Five Social Media Platforms and How to Use Them

There are literally thousands of social media platforms and apps on the market today.

With so many ways to connect with potential customers, focusing your efforts becomes extremely difficult. If you make the mistake of spreading yourself too thin across too many platforms, this wealth of media options will make it harder for you to communicate your brand.

The best *social media strategy* for any new product or new business is to stay focused. Instead of joining every platform you come across, concentrate your forces on one or two of the biggest and most relevant platforms until your following starts to grow exponentially and automatically.

Despite the increasingly high number of social media platforms on the market, there is currently only a handful worth your time and effort—Facebook, Twitter, LinkedIn, Google (YouTube and Google+) and Instagram. These five platforms are referred to as the *Big 5 Social Media Platforms*.

To start promoting your products and brand on social media, pick one of the Big 5 platforms that you understand best and that your audience uses the most. Concentrate your efforts intensely on this one platform. Over time, your following will start to grow. Eventually, your fan base will hit a tipping point to where your most enthusiastic fans will build your platform for you.

Once you have achieved a tipping point with one platform, you can start to concentrate your efforts on a second platform, then a third platform, and so on. Regardless of which of the Big 5 platforms you choose to focus on first, the fastest way to grow it is to understand both how the platform operates and how your audience uses the platform.

This means you need to know the type of content to post on the platform, when to post it, and why you are posting it.

Facebook is best used for posting blog articles, pictures, picture quotes, text quotes, text stories, videos, questions, and polls. The ideal time to post on Facebook is 11 a.m. EST and 6 p.m. EST (these times might vary slightly if you are targeting only certain countries outside of North and South America, the United Kingdom and Europe). More than anything else, people come to Facebook to connect emotionally and visually with others.

Specifically, they come to Facebook to inspire a sense of awe and positive motivation, and to keep tabs on people they have emotional attachments to. Like all social media platforms, Facebook is focusing its efforts heavily on sharing images and, to an even greater extent, sharing live videos.

Instagram, which is now owned by Facebook, is one of the fastest growing social media platforms in the world. No matter your product or overall brand, you should make it a goal to post to Instagram daily. To utilize this platform fully, you should start collating a variety of pictures, picture quotes, picture CTAs (pictures with text and a URL, or an arrow pointing to a hyperlink in the caption), and short fifteen-second videos. Similar to Twitter (see below), there's no use being on Instagram unless you're able to post every few hours between 8 a.m. and 8 p.m. EST. But unlike Twitter, the main reason people come to Instagram is to connect visually with other people. This is why all of your Instagram content should be very visual.

Twitter is best used to share blog articles, text quotes, text quips, complaints, pictures, questions, and answers. There's no use being on Twitter unless you're able to post every few hours between 8 a.m. and 8 p.m. EST. The content turnover on Twitter is so extreme that you should NOT start to build a presence on Twitter unless you can fully commit to it.

More than any other reason, people show up on Twitter to access trending new stories and gossip and to have real-time conversations, share clever observations, and voice harsh criticism. The fastest way to build your presence on Twitter is to start having conversations with disgruntled potential clients. For example, you can reach out to validate someone's frustration with a competitor's product, or to answer someone's question concerning your product.

LinkedIn is best used for posting professional articles, text quotes, training videos, speaking videos, professional questions, and performance surveys. When posting on LinkedIn, as with all other individual social media platforms, make sure that you are tailoring your titles and especially your content overall to that platform's audience and audience behavior.

For example, your blog article might be titled "10 Ways to Help Your Kiddo Deal with a Jerk Bully at School," which would perform very well on Facebook (due to Facebook's more emotional audience behavior) but it may play poorly on LinkedIn due to LinkedIn's less emotional and more professional audience behavior. In this case, a better title might be "10 Tips to Help Your Child Deal with School Bullying."

When posting content on LinkedIn, limit your posts to one to two times per day at 9 a.m., 12 p.m., 3 p.m., 6 p.m. or 9 p.m. EST. LinkedIn is a great platform for increasing brand and product awareness both to potential business partners (business to business, or B2B relationships) and potential end consumers (business to customer, or B2C relationships).

To build these connections, provide other people and businesses with recommendations and positive referrals. The only reason people are on LinkedIn is to promote themselves and their businesses, so the more you can elevate their sense of significance, the more you will build up your LinkedIn presence.

Google owns several social media platforms, including YouTube and Google+. The biggest reason to be active on these platforms is that Google will increase your search ranking in exchange for using their platforms. That's right; by posting content to YouTube (www.youtube.com) and Google+ (www.plus.google.com), you can increase the visibility of your website and overall brand on Google Search. The key is to ensure that these social media platforms are linked up to your website through, for example, a Wordpress plugin, or by adding your site's URL to your Google+ account, or simply by embedding a YouTube video to a blog article on your website.

Once you've grown a strong audience on more than two of these social media platforms, you should start mapping out a plan for automating your content distribution.

Social media management sites like Hootsuite (www.hootsuite.com) allow you to schedule posts on multiple platforms in advance. However, some platforms, such as Facebook, will limit the reach of posts coming through Hootsuite or other third-party social media management sites. Facebook does this to encourage people to create content directly on their site, not on third-party sites.

Regardless of which social media platforms you decide to use, remember that each platform is best used to connect with potential clients, build trust, increase brand awareness, and turn readers, users, followers, and fans into email subscribers.

Remember, content marketing is only creative ownership when you control your own access to the knowledgebase, network, and/or special abilities associated with the content. Don't equate your social media presence to any kind of owner-ship, and don't get addicted to the vanity analytics associated with your social media presence. Instead, stay focused on using social media to expand awareness of your brand and to protect the perception of your brand.

Note

1.   Kissmetrics. '5 reasons email marketing crushes social media market-ing for B2B'. Kissmetrics Blog. https://blog.kissmetrics.com/email-crushes-social-media/

24 The Laws of Convergence, Replication, and Accelerated Returns

It is in the nature of exponential growth that events develop extremely slowly for extremely long periods of time, but as one glides through the knee of the curve, events erupt at an increasingly furious pace.

—Ray Kurzweil

Now that you understand what it takes to be a creative owner, you're ready to start replicating and scaling your means of ownership. The key is to start thinking of your efforts as one giant, automated funnel.

You will bring attention into this funnel through social media, blog posts, lead magnets, and other forms of content. Then, as the sources of this attention diverge down a sales funnel, you will consistently track and analyze where in the funnel people exit (fail to buy your product or opt-out in general), and why.

Over time, you will repair more and more of these "leaks" in your funnel until it is generating high levels of sales conversions, as well as elevated levels of cash flow and profits.

Once your first sales funnel is completely automated and generating positive income, you will need to meticulously evaluate its key metrics, such as Customer Lifetime Value, Customer Profitability, and Customer Acquisition Cost.

As you continue down the path of being a successful entre-employee, you will need to continually elevate your levels of ownership. To do this, you will need to invest heavily in innovating new products, new product funnels, and new lifestyle businesses. When scaling your efforts in this way, make sure you take advantage of the laws of *convergence*, *replication*, and *acceleration*.

What is the Law of Convergence?

The law of convergence states, "All effective content will be repackaged into two or more other pieces of content." The blogosphere and the internet, in general, is a hungry beast. You have to feed this monster continuously.

If you don't, the monster will stop bringing new readers, users, followers, and fans to you.

Worse, someone else may repackage your content and use it for their own purposes.

The only way to continue to scale and stay ahead of the competition is to repackage your best content. Text-based blog posts and articles should be repackaged into eBooks and eventually product documents. Podcasts, blog videos, and webinars should be repackaged into video training series and online courses.

When you video record yourself interviewing someone as part of a live webinar, you should repackage the webinar into an online course, then use the video portion as a video blog or training video, then repackage the audio portion of the webinar and use it as a podcast, and then repackage the audio file into a text blog using a transcription app such as Rev.com.

Do *not* make the mistake of building up a robust content library and letting all of your best books sit on the shelves. Instead, pull the books down and *repackage, repackage*, and *repackage* some more.

What is the Law of Replication?

The law of replication states, "It is easier to replicate a working sales funnel than it is to create a new working funnel."

In other words, it's easier to reproduce a sales funnel that is already working, even one that might appear boring to you, than it is to create a new funnel for a very innovative product.

The purpose of this law is to prevent you from going off on a wild goose chase for every great idea you have for a new product, or a new brand, or a new business. As an entre-employee, you're wired to start new ventures but you may lack the follow through needed to finish what you start.

Once you build a funnel that works, as defined by profits and positive cash flow, the fastest and most effective way to expand your efforts and increase your cash flow further is to use that exact same funnel for a new segment of your readership and market, or for a whole new market altogether.

For example, if you're using an eBook to capture leads for a six-part webinar series product and the funnel is working well, your next funnel should use an eBook as its lead capture and a six-part webinar series as its product. Of course, innovation is a necessary component of any successful brand, but replicating what is already working deserves your time and energy too.

By following the laws of convergence and replication, you will achieve the law of accelerated returns, which states: "All efforts that result in achieving a particular goal will be amplified exponentially once an effective system for achieving that goal has been put in place."

Systemization is a vital part of the laws of convergence and replication. Without effective systemization, converging and replicating your efforts will become impossible and, as a result, scaling your efforts will too. However, with efficient systems in place (an effective content marketing system, an effective product launch system, and effective fulfillment system) you can start to accelerate your results.

You now know how to relieve yourself of dependence by creating content, building a brand, and establishing trust with potential clients. You also know how to drive potential customers to you, turn them into email subscribers, and convert them into paying customers.

Overall, you know what it takes to become a successful entre-employee, setting yourself up for a lifetime of ownership, not dependence. The rest of this book focuses on developing a pragmatic mindset and leveraging the power of consistent, practical action to attain *Intelligent Achievement*.

Case Study #4: Franco Valentino

Don't go on vacation, bring the vacation to your living room.

Franco Valentino learned the hard way that he was only one bad phone call away from his life changing forever.

Franco had worked at IBM as a program manager. He did the corporate thing for a decade without ever thinking there was much else out there. Franco was living a pretty good life and, as he put it, "that was okay for now." But then "for now" turned into ten years of mediocrity.

Every day at his office, Franco would fantasize about running his own business. He would take his one and only vacation every year and travel to Las Vegas or the Caribbean, or somewhere else—anywhere else. But instead of enjoying his time off, he would play out how his life might be (or might have been) over and over.

The endless possibilities stretched out before him each work day, making it easier to get through the hours but even harder to come back to work the next morning.

Then, Franco got a call.

One of his children was sick. Very sick.

Franco needed to take care of his family, but he also needed to bring in his paycheck. His job didn't allow him to work from home. There were no other options. He was caught in the middle of an impossible equation. Ultimately, Franco chose to put his family first.

Franco's finances took a dive, and he burned through his savings. Eventually, he had to leave IBM. It was a harsh lesson. But unlike a lot of people, Franco learned it well. He knew that he needed to build a business or platform for himself. He needed to stop being dependent on only one source of income and a single professional network. He needed to become a creative owner.

This wasn't just a self-serving desire, though. Franco needed to do this so he could take care of his family no matter what happened.

Franco needed to do this so he could leave a legacy behind him—something that would protect and provide for his family long after he was gone.

Something that would serve others long after he was gone.

Something that shouted, "I was here and built this, and people are better because of it!"

The problem was Franco didn't know where to start. He tried a few things but fumbled around for a few years, struggling to support his family and learn all the pieces of creating something valuable—something other people needed and that resonated with him. As a network engineer, Franco had always enjoyed programming software apps and optimizing websites.

Over the years, Franco had noticed that the average person had no idea how to optimize a website to rank highly on Google and other search engines. Almost no one knew how important website speed was to a site's Google ranking or the importance of an SSL certificate. That's when Franco decide to launch a new platform and service for small businesses called Website Ecosystems.

Franco identified a need in the market and then developed an offering to meet that need. Over time, he aligned this need and his offer, which created a powerful voice for his platform. Now, Franco helps both small businesses and large corporations develop faster loading websites that rank highly on search engines, and he does it all from his home, on his terms.

Website Ecosystems continues to grow, and Franco continues to automate the company's services. He has used the laws of convergence, replication, and accelerated returns to repeat these results over and over again with many different companies. As a result, Franco generates 58% of his income passively. Now, Franco doesn't just go on vacation once a year. Instead, he vacations daily because Franco's business brings the vacation to his living room every morning, and every day, and every night while he sleeps.

A few months ago, Franco was traveling to give a talk when he got another phone call. Another family member was sick. As expected, Franco's emotions ran high. But in a sense, Franco felt a sense of peace. He could be there for his family this time, without sacrificing his job and financial security.

Part 3
Pragmatic Growth

Dream in a pragmatic way.

—Aldous Huxley

P ragmatic change is lasting. You are responsible for your life, the good and the bad; and, while you cannot dramatically change your life overnight, there are opportunities you can seize daily to bring you to the pinnacle of *Intelligent Achievement*. Pragmatic growth is the key to seizing the right opportunity at the right time without sacrificing personal responsibility.

25 Turning Pain into Productivity Through Pragmatism

We are hard pressed on every side, but not crushed; perplexed, but not in despair; persecuted, but not abandoned; struck down, but not destroyed.

—Paul the Apostle (2 Corinthians 4:8–9 NIV)

Trauma hurts. Tragedy, by definition, is painful.

After my diagnosis, I was put on a medical surveillance plan that involved routine blood tests and CT scans (see the Preface for the backstory). This meant that I could never get away from what happened. I couldn't escape it.

Every month, when I walked into the medical center to get blood drawn, I was reminded. My life at the time rose and fell in 30-day increments. Every month before the blood draw, my stress levels would rise and I would become impatient with those around me. The day before the blood draw, my nerves would calm, and I would become peaceful and present.

When the blood results came back normal, I would feel free and light and strangely proud of myself. I would relax and float through life patiently, being kind to everyone in my path. Then the cycle would start over again.

The pain of being kept on edge by these tests was chronic and immense. At first, I didn't know how to handle it. I didn't know how to live. I felt like I was carrying a very heavy weight with nowhere to let the weight rest. My stress built and built and built because I lacked a clear outlet for it.

Finally, one day, while sitting alone in a public garden by my house, I figured out the problem—I was focusing on everything that could go wrong. If I wanted to feel better about my life, and if I actually wanted to make my life better, I would need to start focusing on the positive changes available to me. What small, practical step could I take right now to improve my life? What tiny, mini-habit could I implement to start turning me into the person I had always wanted to become?

The key to changing my focus was making small, pragmatic decisions followed by even smaller, pragmatic actions. Slowly, I gained control and slowly my life got better and better until going to the doctor became my road to success instead of a weight I had to carry.

Transform Pain Through Pragmatic Thinking

Your mindset defines your point of view, or the way you look at the world. If you're always looking at things from a limited viewpoint—you don't have enough time, you're too old, you're too busy—you'll always have a limited attitude, and you'll always be in pain.

Likewise, if you're always taking on too much at once—inflating what is logically possible for you to achieve or succumbing to every desire that presents itself—you'll always feel behind, overwhelmed, and out of control. As a result, you'll always be in pain.

The only way to relieve this pain is to transform your mindset.

You must develop a pragmatic mindset.

You must become a *pragmatist*.

A pragmatic mindset will ensure that you stay in touch with reality while always maintaining a sense of personal responsibility in your life. A pragmatic mindset will also increase your *resilience*, which is the key to overcoming the pain associated with trauma, tragedy, or adversity.

Studies reported by the American Psychological Association confirm that people who have a pragmatic mindset are more resilient; and resilient people, when faced with stress, are measurably happier than those who are not resilient.[1] The same studies showed that resilient people, in turn, have a more stable state of mind overall.

Pragmatism is about protecting your mindset, and protecting yourself against unwanted thoughts and desires is essential for goal attainment. Research from the *Personality and Social Psychology Bulletin* agrees that if you don't strategically protect yourself from damaging internal influences by controlling your mindset, you are more likely to sabotage your success.[2]

Have you ever pulled back right before reaching a big goal? Have you ever refused to ask for help and tried, unsuccessfully, to do everything yourself? Have you ever overthought a situation and, as a result, failed to make the right decision? This is *self-sabotage* and it is the result of impractical thinking.

A scientific study in the *Journal of Applied Psychology* looked at personality and goal-striving and found that a person's mindset emerged as the most important aspect of the self-regulation process and an important motivational strategy that successful people use while working toward goal achievement.[3]

Your mindset today will control where you end up tomorrow.

Science shows that when a pragmatic mindset is maintained, goals get achieved, and people feel an increased sense of well-being and improved mood, as well as an increased ability to select, set, and achieve future goals.

Maintaining a pragmatic mindset will protect you against threats of both internal and external distraction. By learning to think pragmatically, you'll notice an increase in self-reliance, internal motivation, and commitment to your goals, which will make transforming pain into productivity an easy job to accomplish.

How to Use Your Negativity Bias to Your Advantage

Your brain has a *negativity bias*—it has a preference for negative information over positive information.

Studies show that negative information is quickly routed through your amygdala and into your long-term memory

banks while positive information has to be held in your awareness for more than 12 seconds to be stored in your long-term
memory banks.[4]

This is why you will remember forever the one negative
comment your boss made during your performance review,
but will instantly forget the fifteen positive comments he
made before and after. This is also why someone cutting
you off in traffic or failing to hold the elevator for you on
the way to work can ruin your entire day but someone
smiling at you and saying "hello" or "thank you" barely
alters your mood.

What if you started using this negativity bias to your
advantage?

What if you leveraged everything that happened to
you, the good and the bad, into meaningful action? The key
is always to channel your mental energy into productive
action—not just talk or, worse, complaints.

No matter what happens to you, there's no value in complaining about it. Complaining only makes things worse.

A study in the journal *Developmental Psychology* reported
by the American Psychological Association found that people
who vent to one another about their problems for extended
periods of time are more likely to develop depression and
anxiety.[5] Moreover, when you whine, you encourage other
people to do it too.

Whining attracts whiny people.

If you complain long enough, you'll start to get pulled
into other people's conflicts. Whether it's a friend calling
to complain, some troll baiting you on social media, or a

colleague sending you a passive-aggressive email, you'll dive headfirst into the drama. You can't wait to mix things up and prove you're right. But, by doing so, you let these cynical and manipulative people win.

When mistakes, failures, and frustrating events happen, the only way to leverage them to your advantage is to regain control of your mindset, and start transforming your pain into productivity. Do not fall into the trap of complaining about the negative event or allowing other people to complain about it.

Instead, channel all of your mental energy into positive, pragmatic action. When something goes wrong, take action. When someone else complains about their life, ignore them and take action in your own life. This will ensure that all the pain you experience in life does not go to waste but instead, is used to move you forward towards *Intelligent Achievement*.

Notes

1. Flynn, F. 'If you need help, just ask: Underestimating compliance with direct requests for help'. *Journal of Personality and Social Psychology*, 95(1): 128–143. http://psycnet.apa.org/journals/emo/9/3/361/

2. Achtziger, A. *et al.* (2008) 'Implementation intentions and shielding goal striving from unwanted thoughts and feelings'. *Personality and Psychology Bulletin, 34*(3). http://journals.sagepub.com/doi/abs/10.1177/0146167207311201

3. Lee, F. K. (2003) 'Personality and the goal-striving process: the influence of achievement goal patterns, goal level, and mental focus on performance and enjoyment'. *Journal of Applied Psychology.* 88(2): 256–65. https://www.ncbi.nlm.nih.gov/pubmed/12731709

4. Hanson, R. 'How your brain makes you feel intimidated'. *Confronting the Negativity Bias.* http://www.rickhanson.net/how-your-brain-makes-you-easily-intimidated/

5. APA (2007) 'Someone to complain with isn't necessarily a good thing, especially for teenage girls'. http://www.apa.org/news/press/releases/2007/07/co-rumination.aspx

26 One Non-Negotiable is Worth a Thousand To-Dos

On this subject, I do not wish to think, or to speak, or write, with moderation … I will not equivocate—I will not excuse—I will not retreat a single inch.

—William Lloyd Garrison

In graduate school, I loved creating lists. I would write and rewrite lists of journal articles to read, experiments to do, people to network with, and workout routines to complete at night.

Every time I created a new list, I felt really productive, like I had just created something concrete, something that moved me one step closer to accomplishing my goals.

Of course, I never read any of the articles on the list; I only did the experiments I was told to do; and, once, I showed up to the gym and did the same workout routine I had been doing for years.

Every Sunday, I would spend an hour writing a list of 50 tasks to complete during the week. Then, I would stare blankly at the monster I just created, put the list aside, and continue checking my email and scrolling through my Facebook feed.

Eventually, I realized that these to-do lists never resulted in practical results. Worse, they were reducing my productivity levels and damaging my initiative. Not only was creating these massive lists wasting significant amounts of my mental energy, but the infinite number of tasks on each list was also inhibiting my brain from deciding on which to complete.

To-Do Lists are Time-Wasters

Action items are rarely actionable. The greater the options you have, the fewer the decisions you are likely to make. The same holds true for your to-do list. The more action items you write on a piece of paper, the less likely you are to decide on any one of them and the less likely you are to take action.

Bullet points kill dreams. Writing down an endless list of action items encourages tactical over strategic thinking and prevents forward progress. There are three scientific reasons why to-do lists limit success. The first is that the average to-do list exhibits heterogeneous complexity.[1]

In other words, the list contains some tasks that will take ten seconds to complete, some that will take ten minutes to complete, and some that will take ten hours to complete. The average person will automatically focus on crossing off the ten-second tasks so they can receive, as soon as possible, the psychological payoff and dopamine release that comes with it. This means that tedious, yet important tasks (like writing a business proposal or completing the first chapter of your book), will stay on the list for a very long time.

The second reason why to-do lists limit success is that the average to-do list displays heterogeneous priority.[2]

Most to-do lists lack both context and hierarchy. This means the tasks that are most important to you "right now" will take top priority, even if they are a low priority overall. Simultaneously, the tasks themselves do not provide any information about the best time to complete the task or how long each will take.

The third reason why to-do lists prevent success is that they offer too many options. In *The Art of Choosing*,[3] Sheena Iyengar, a professor at Columbia University, discusses a study she conducted in a California supermarket. Professor Iyengar and her team set up a sample booth offering little cups of Wilkin & Sons jam.[4]

Every hour or two, the team switched from offering a selection of six jams to a selection of 24 jams. Regardless of the size of the assortment, the average customer tasted only two jams.

However, 30% of the people who had sampled from the small assortment decided to buy jam while only 3% of the people who had sampled from the large assortment decided to buy. Offering four times as many choices reduced sales tenfold.

How to Leverage the Power of "No"

To-do lists dismantle productivity. Learning to say "no," on the other hand, protects productivity. Saying "no" also helps you prioritize.

The fastest way to figure out what's important to you is first to know what's *not* important to you. (Just like every failed relationship you've ever had has taught you what you do *not* want in a partner more than it taught you what you do want.)

This is true in even the smallest matters of life. For example, I may not know what I want for dinner, but I definitely know what I do *not* want for dinner. This process of elimination helps narrow down what really matters from what really doesn't.

Do you know when to say "no"?

Do you recognize what you do *not* need in your life?

If not, it's time to gain an intimate understanding of the magical two-letter word, "no." This one, simple word can eliminate a lot of problems from your life.

The problem is you've likely been encouraged to only say "no" to things that are unhealthy or dangerous. But being unable to say "no", even to healthy things, is linked to increased overwhelm, stress, and lack of productivity.

Saying "no" is pragmatic.

This is because "no" is scientifically proven to enhance self-control and self-preservation. The University of Nottingham published a meta-analysis of 83 studies showing that saying "no" increased self-control over destructive, unhealthy, or wasteful activities, increased successful goal attainment, and protection against decision fatigue.[5] Conversely, the same study linked lapses in the ability to say "no" to a host of social and behavioral issues.

A second study published in the *Journal of Consumer Research* reinforced the fact that saying "no" is critical to reaching your goals in life.[6] However, the study found that it's not just *that* you say "no," it's *how* you say "no" that matters.

Side-stepping conflict and other *passive avoidance* techniques like saying "I can't" instead of "no" or "I don't want to" will not help you achieve your goals any faster. In fact, refusing to say "no" firmly and directly was found to be disempowering and inversely proportional to goal attainment.

So, if saying "no" is the secret to success, why do so few people choose to say it?

A Columbia University study in the *Journal of Personality and Social Psychology* reveals that saying "no" causes stress and is interpreted by the brain as a negative event due to a complex mixture of fear of rejection, fear of hurting someone's feelings, and fear of disconnection.[7]

Very simply, we don't say "no" because we are afraid.

We're afraid to lose respect, connection, and acceptance. The anticipation of this can be more influential in making a decision than anything positive that might be gained. As a result, most people just shrivel up and say "yes" because it feels safer at the time.

The key to saying "no" more is realizing the practical cost of saying "yes" too much. When you overcommit and let people push you around with their agendas, you damage your self-confidence and self-integrity. You also move yourself further and further from your goals.

The solution is simple—maintain a pragmatic mindset. Anything you lose by saying "no" once can easily be attained by saying "yes" in the future and, if it can't, it wasn't worth having in the first place.

Going Beyond "No" to "Never Again" and "Non-Negotiable"

Once you start saying "no" to the things you don't want, you'll be able to see the things you do want more clearly.

What is valuable in your life right now?

How are you going to protect this value?

The answer is *not* by saying "yes" to more and more things. Instead, the only way to permanently protect what is truly important to you is to go beyond "no" to "never again."

A *non-negotiable* is simply something you will never compromise. The word "never" has irresistible force. But you have to mean it. You have to take it seriously and never, ever break it. If you take them seriously, you can use non-negotiables to organize and prioritize your day.

Bookending your days with non-negotiables is a proven way to infuse yourself with greater focus and a greater sense of urgency throughout the day. For example, you're *never* going to skip waking up at 7 a.m. to go to the gym. (This is bookend number one.) And, you're *never* going to stay online past 9:30 p.m. (This is bookend number two.)

Once you bookmark the beginning and ending of your days, you can add additional bookmarks throughout your day. You're *never* going to check your phone before lunch and risk the possibility of getting sucked into a friend's drama. Or, you're *never* going to check email more than once a day.

There's real freedom in refusing to compromise on yourself. Taking a hard stance in your life with a handful of non-negotiables will force you to work within strict, pragmatic boundaries, which will, in turn, allow you to use your sense of urgency to your advantage. It will also enable you to align your most important tasks with your peak hours of mental energy.

Notes

1. Abu-Asab, M., *et al.* (2012) 'Analyzing heterogeneous complexity in complementary and alternative medicine research: a systems biology solution via parsimony phylogenetics'. *Forsch Komplementmed. 1*: 42–8. doi: 10.1159/000335190. https://www.ncbi.nlm.nih.gov/pubmed/22327551

2. Viswanathan, A. and Rama Murthy, G. 'Heterogeneous dynamic priority scheduling in time critical applications: Mobile Wireless Sensor Networks'. Thesis. https://arxiv.org/abs/1302.5903

3. Iyengar, S. (2011). *The art of choosing*. New York: Twelve. https://www.amazon.com/The-Art-Choosing-Sheena-Iyengar/dp/0446504114

4. Wilkin & Sons. 'Tiptree jams and preserves'. https://www.tiptree.com

5. Hagger, M. S., *et al.* (2010) 'Ego depletion and the strength model of self-control: a meta-analysis'. *Psychology Bulletin. 136*(4): 495–525. https://www.ncbi.nlm.nih.gov/pubmed/20565167

6. Patrick, V. and Hagtvedt, H. (2012) '"I don't" versus "I can't": When empowered refusal motivates goal-directed behavior'. *Journal of Consumer Research, 39*(2): 371–381 http://www.jstor.org/stable/10.1086/663212?seq=1#page_scan_tab_contents

7. Flynn, F. *et al.* (2008) 'If you need help, just ask: Underestimating compliance with direct requests for help'. *Journal of Personality and Social Psychology, 95*(1): 128–143. http://dx.doi.org/10.1037/0022–3514.95.1.128

27 The Real Theory of Relativity and the Law of Relaxed Productivity

Efficiency is doing things right; effectiveness is doing the right things.

—Peter Drucker

I used to get wildly frustrated at my boss, especially after a long day at work. I would fantasize about throwing everything off of my desk, kicking his office door open, and yelling "Hey, fool—I quit!"

Of course, these fantasies took on various forms with harsher language on the really bad days ...

One day, I realized that there was a pattern to my frustration. I noticed that I would get fired up and have this quitting fantasy at the end of my work days, not at the beginning.

When I had a day full of pointless meetings, these fantasies would happen earlier in the day.

There was a method to the madness in my head. Once I discovered my mental pattern, I started pushing my lunch breaks back to later in the day (and secretly extending them a bit). I went for a run or went to the gym during these breaks. Sometimes I just went for a long walk. This made all the difference, and my "frustration cycle" (as I like to call it) was reset.

Why did these simple changes help me improve my life? How did they help me improve my life?

Your World is Relative to Your Mood, Focus and Motivation

In today's world, staying peaceful and practical is exceptionally hard. Everyone in your life is vying for your attention. Everyone is trying to arouse you to take action on their behalf. This includes your boss, your spouse, television commercials, pop-up ads, your close friends, beggars on the street, and even me right now (again, thanks for reading). Studies show that every unit of your attention that you give away to one of these factors depresses your mood, focus, and motivation.

The real theory of relativity is as follows: *The meaning you give to your experiences is relative to your mood, focus, and motivation during those experiences.*

A study published in the journal *Chronobiology International* found that the mind and body go through rhythms of emotion, alertness, and energy.[1] One simple example of such a rhythm is the dip in motivation you and most people feel after eating lunch and returning to work. The above study went on to find that patterns in performance and focus were governed more by numerous individual factors than generalized ones.

In other words, emotional states and energy levels varied greatly depending on the person and the circumstance.

As a result, how frustrating a particular incident seems, or how difficult an individual task seems, or how good or bad your overall day seems is all relative to your mood, focus, and motivation levels.

The Three Non-Relative Relativity Exceptions in Life

Not everything is relative. While your world is often defined by the upswing or downswing of your mindset, including your mood, focus, and motivation levels, some influential factors are consistent regardless of person or circumstance.

The *Journal of Biological Rhythms* found that, regardless of any relative emotional, mental, physiological, or time-based influences (including sleep), peak performance is consistently influenced by three factors.[2]

These three factors are—you guessed it—mood, focus, and motivation.

So, while your emotions, focus, and overall motivation will vary based on who you are and on your personal circumstances, they will still *always* affect your performance. In other words, no matter who you are or what your baseline levels are, *elevating* your mood, focus, and motivation will *increase* your performance.

Did you catch that?

I just shared the answer to the game of life.

No matter what you're trying to achieve, the only three things that you can always count on to improve your performance are your mood, focus, and motivation.

But what's the point?

Why should you or anyone want to know what's relative in life and what's not relative? The answer is so that you can learn how to be exceedingly productive in life and supremely relaxed in life at the same time.

Anyone can be extremely productive and stressed out of their mind at the same time. (I pulled off this particular feat for years until my health crisis.) Others can be transcendently relaxed and happy without ever being productive (they're called hippies).

A genuine sign of an enlightened mind and sophisticated life is to be both productive and relaxed at the same time. But is this actually possible?

The Law of Relaxed Productivity and How to Follow it

The law of relaxed productivity states: the more effective your process is, the more productive you will be. The more efficient your process is, the more relaxed you will be.

The key to being productive and relaxed at the same time is to be as effective and efficient as possible at the same time.

Again, anyone can be either effective or efficient; few can do both simultaneously. Let's look at an example from Abraham Lincoln.

Lincoln once wrote, "Give me six hours to chop down a tree and I will spend the first four sharpening the axe." What did he mean by this? What is this statement meant to teach? Why was balancing the time spent sharpening and the time spent chopping important? The answer lies in balancing effectiveness with efficiency.

Let's say swinging the ax consistently to hit the tree in the same spot over and over again is a measure of efficiency, while the number of times the ax is swung before the tree finally falls is a measure of effectiveness.

The more consistently the ax is swung, the more efficient the ax swinger is. The fewer times the ax is swung, the more effective the ax swinger is.

An efficient but ineffective person will sharpen the ax briefly and spend the majority of their time swinging consistently against the tree in the same spot. The amount of time they spend sharpening the ax doesn't matter in this case because the ax swinger is going for maximum efficiency only.

An effective but inefficient person, on the other hand, will sharpen the ax for nearly the full six hours and then hack away like mad at the tree to chop it down in a few minutes (possibly cutting off their leg or giving themselves a heart attack in the process).

Lincoln would do things differently. Lincoln, as mentioned, would spend the first four hours sharpening his ax (to allow for effective chopping) and the last two cutting down the tree (to allow for efficient chopping). This shows that, in the mind of Lincoln, both effectiveness and efficiency are necessary for peak performance. It also shows that Lincoln favors effectiveness over efficiency 2:1 when it comes to performing well.

If you follow Lincoln's practical model of peak performance—valuing both effectiveness and efficiency but favoring the former 2:1—you will not only excel in every area of your life, you will perfectly follow the law of being relaxed and productive at the same time. This balance between effectiveness and efficiency is at the heart of pragmatic action. A pragmatist is not an extremist. A pragmatist is someone who leverages the right method in the right way, and at the right time, to achieve the right results.

Notes

1. Carrier, J. and Monk, T. H. (2000) 'Circadian rhythms of performance: new trends'. *Chronobiology International.* *17*(6): 719–32. https://www.ncbi.nlm.nih.gov/pubmed/11128289

2. Hull, J. T., Wright, K.P. and Czeisler, C. A. (2003) 'The influence of subjective alertness and motivation on human performance independent of circadian and homeostatic regulation'. *Journal of Biological Rhythms*, *18*(4): 329–38. https://www.ncbi.nlm.nih.gov/pubmed/12932085

28 Avoiding Drama, FOMO, and "Blind Spot Ignorance"

Self-justification is a treacherous servant.

— Wellington Mara

As you've learned in previous chapters, mental energy is your most valuable asset. The key to protecting your mental energy is being pragmatic with how you spend it.

This means avoiding the slow drip, drip, drip of allowing drama and other distractions to endlessly drain your mental energy levels.

Why is drama so alluring?

The reason is because drama makes people feel important. Either they feel important because they created something that attracts attention, or they feel important because they get to save the day by rushing in to fix someone else's problem.

Only people with small, insignificant goals are drawn to drama. Finally! Something that matters! Something I can solve! Someone I can save!

The truth is that the drama you or other people choose to engage in isn't important. It's just another distraction. It's another way for you to kill time before your meaningless, boring life ends.

The hard truth is you don't care (and shouldn't care) about other people's meaningless dramas. All you care about is how trying to save the day makes you look and feel. Drama makes you feel important. But this feeling is fake. It's self-absorbed. It's worthless. Stop engaging in drama. Instead, get some better problems. Start choosing some more worthy challenges to take on.

What is FOMO and Who has it?

Do you ever feel a deep sense of guilt or dread over missing out on an "important" meeting or opportunity?

If so, you likely have FOMO.

Feeling like you're about to miss out on something is too painful for most people—so much so that pop culture has dubbed this pain as FOMO, or the fear-of-missing-out.

Remember, your mind hates pain. So, when your colleague invites you to a meeting or tells you about his million-dollar idea, or when your boss asks for volunteers to work late on a special project, your mind will feel the urge to jump at this "opportunity" to avoid the pain of missing out. The only way to overcome your FOMO is to start ignoring the urge to be a part of everything.

Start building up a resistance against it by practicing saying "no" to initial offers. As mentioned previously, you should never fall into the trap of thinking that you have only one chance to say "yes." In most cases, you can say "no" to an opportunity at first and say "yes" later. Likewise, you can say "no" to an opportunity that you *already* said "yes" to.

Of course, it's important to be accountable to your commitments, but not all commitments must last forever. If you change your mind or grow out of a responsibility, don't be afraid to talk about it openly and find a better way forward.

How Selective "Blind Spot Ignorance" Leads to Disaster

Personality and Social Sciences Bulletin published a study showing that people are better able to point out cognitive blind spots or perceptual biases in others, but struggle to identify those same blind spots in themselves.[1]

Then, despite test scores that proved their biased perception, these people were still either unable or unwilling to recognize their blind spots. In other words, they actively chose to evade reality and live in ignorance. This is something I have experienced first-hand.

A few years ago, I thought I had it all figured out. I was going to be rich. Blind positivity flooded my senses. A few years ago, when I was starting my first business, I invested everything into a product without doing any market research.

I liked the product, I liked working on it, and that was enough to keep me happy. But this happiness didn't last. Eventually, this creeping sense of dread trickled into my life. And it grew and grew and grew. I knew both the product and the business were going to fail before I even finished developing the product. But I was too invested to quit.

So I kept on investing, irrationally. I created a fog around my feelings and around any information that contradicted the blind hope that my business would be successful. In short, I completely evaded reality.

Despite every metric and every piece of feedback I received telling me not to launch, I launched the product anyway. No one bought it. No one noticed it. It bombed. I failed, and now I was broke.

This was when I realized that being blindly positive in life, by itself, is a mistake. Instead, you have to be exceptionally positive but also have the guts to look reality in the face and make shrewd judgments based on the feedback reality gives you.

The truth is, everyone's a hypocrite at some point, in some way—we just often lack the insight to recognize it. The problem with any self-justification is that it distracts you from reality. Self-justification makes you feel better in the moment but keeps you from growing.

Over time, you don't just distort the present, you distort the past; until all you remember is the personal script of near-fiction that suits your unwillingness to change. Self-perception and social perception are rarely congruent, according to a paper published in *Psychological Review*.[2]

Not surprisingly, we attribute more validity to OUR perceptions and judgments of others and ourselves than to other people's opinions and judgments of us.

When you lack insight and honest self-evaluation, it's easy to be led down the wrong path. It's easy to be held hostage in the same bad job or same bad relationship. Instead of doing the hard work to change these situations, most people disengage. A scientific study in *Personality and Social Psychology Bulletin* refers to this ego defense mechanism as "adaptive disengagement."[3]

If you feel you can't ever change, if you feel you can't grow and become better, you'll employ bias to avoid changing. In short, you'll lie to yourself. Lying to yourself is the cardinal sin which defeats pragmatism.

Distorting reality instead of engaging directly with it always has an unpleasant reckoning.

The only way to prevent this reckoning is to look directly at your failures, your shortcomings, your secrets, your vices … everything. Be pragmatic and take personal responsibility for everything in your life because it's all your fault. This sounds harsh, but only by taking responsibility can you start improving your situation.

Two Keys to Keeping Your Blind Spots in Full View

Keeping your blind spots in plain view comes down to two things: first, an ability to be ruthlessly honest with yourself, and second, maintaining a higher standard for yourself than others set for you. Ruthlessness is a valuable trait.

Ask yourself, when was the last time you were really honest with yourself?

Painfully honest …

It's great to be confident and focus on your strengths all the time. It's necessary for success. But to exist permanently in a state of blind positivity can keep you from growing. You don't get a free pass in life for being positive. No one is coming to give you a ribbon just for showing up and smiling like a buffoon. Instead, you're going to have to do the tough work of identifying your shortcomings, mistakes, and biases.

You are going to have to get courageous and take a hard look at your dark side. You're going to have to take a look at yourself using a wider lens.

What are you ignoring in yourself because you're too afraid to face it? What traits, habits, thought addictions or behaviors have you indulged in and rationalized because you never feel ready to change them?

Maybe you've excused yourself because you think change is impossible.

"But this is just who I am."

Cringe.

What a cop-out.

And, it's scientifically untrue.

People can and do change—it's a fact. They do it all the time.

Start looking at what you know you need to change in your life. Start looking at which of your routine thoughts and actions make you feel bad about yourself.

Be honest with your shortcomings and where you've made mistakes. Once you've looked hard at these blind spots, sit with them. Sit with the pain of realizing you're not perfect. Then, make the decision to change.

Once you get ruthlessly honest, you need to set a much higher standard for yourself. Now that you've faced your demons head on, take action. Make hard decisions. Set a higher bar for yourself.

Get surgical with the garbage people and garbage activities in your life. Cut them out and refuse to let them creep back into your focus and existence forever. Excise the negative.

Most importantly, own your mistakes. Take responsibility for your shortcomings and stop making excuses. You are to blame for everything in your life. You are the source of your reactions. You can't control everything that happens to you, but you can control how you respond.

It doesn't matter what contributed to any of your pitfalls—you get to decide how you use them (or let them use you), moving forward. Own up to the bad mistakes and poor judgments you've made in your life. Accept accountability for your actions and their ripple effect on yourself, your progress, and people around you.

Think back to the business deal you should have rejected, the job you hated but held onto for too long, the relationship you let wear you down, and every other part of your life that you should have let go of a long time ago: they need to be confronted.

Now, ask yourself, what decisions will you make next time to avoid repeated mistakes?

What questions will you ask in advance for the next job, business deal, or relationship?

What impulses will you notice within yourself that might lead you down wrong paths that you can circumvent going forward?

How will you be more pragmatic next time?

Get out of your own way by accepting that you've made bad choices. Then take heart in the fact that every bad choice is an opportunity to learn and grow. You can't grow in fantasyland. You can't grow by ignoring your blind spots. You can only grow by facing reality, keeping your blind spots in full view, and taking pragmatic action, which will lead to lasting growth.

Notes

1. Pronin, E., Lin, D. and Lin, L. R. (2002) 'The bias blind spot: Perceptions of bias in self versus others'. *Personality and Social Psychology Bulletin,* 28(3). http://journals.sagepub.com/doi/abs/10.1177/0146167202286008

2. Pronin, E., Gilovich, T. and Ross L. (2004) 'Objectivity in the eye of the beholder: divergent perceptions of bias in self versus others'. *Psychological Review.* 111(3): 781–99. https://www.ncbi.nlm.nih.gov/pubmed/15250784

3. Leitner, J. B., Hehman, E. and Deegan M. (2014) 'Adaptive disengagement buffers self-esteem from negative social feedback'. http://journals.sagepub.com/doi/abs/10.1177/0146167214549319

29 Preventing the Deadly Eight Productivity Pitfalls

Productivity is not just about doing more. It is about creating more impact with less work.

—Prerna Malik

After working with thousands of people all over the world, I've been able to identify certain patterns in the way people think and act. I've also been able to determine the most common distractions that keep the average person from being more productive. These "Deadly Eight Productivity Pitfalls" are as follows:

1. Accepting free handouts

2. Having a variable morning routine

3. Putting small priorities first

4. Avoiding difficult but important tasks

5. Following the eight-hour work day

6. Checking their phone constantly

7. Replying to emails immediately

8. Overcommitting to favors

Unproductive people love gifts. They love free handouts. If you want to start being more productive, you need to start refusing free handouts from other people no matter how well-meaning.

There's no such thing as a free lunch. The law of reciprocity[1] prevents it. Under this law, you can never take anything from anyone without feeling a strong urge to give them something in return.

This desire to give back to someone who gives you something, even if you don't want or need what they're giving you, is intensely distracting. The only way to stay focused and productive is to be very deliberate with what you accept from people.

This includes praise. For example, if your boss praises you for your good work, be careful how much weight you give his praise because it could make you feel like you have to say "yes" to working next weekend. Instead, keep praise in its place.

Own it, but don't rely on it or feel like you have to live up to it by blindly saying "yes" to something in return.

Unproductive people change their minds often. Unproductive people struggle to keep any kind of schedule. The problem with never keeping a schedule or never sticking with a routine is that each time you vary from the routine, you have to make a decision on what to do next.

These decisions reduce your mental energy stores. Remember, you only have so much willpower each day. You have a set number of willpower units you can use. Once your willpower units are used up, your mind is weak. You'll make bad decisions.

Like eating a whole box of cookies before bed. Or staying out late Friday night after a hard week at the office. I know—it happens. The best strategy for avoiding decision fatigue is to fill your life with healthy habits.

Unproductive people are also horrible at prioritization. If you want to start being more productive, you need to start prioritizing. You need to start organizing your day sequentially based on your top priorities. Most people are unhappy because their priorities were passively set by a hodgepodge of subconscious beliefs.

These people say that success, career, family, relationships, health, or happiness are most important. Then they spend all of their mental energy on pointless activities like surfing the web, checking emails, going to pointless meetings, and playing on their phones.

What you spend the most mental energy on is your top priority. You might say something noble is your priority. You might think it's your top priority. But if you're not spending most of your mental energy on it—guess what?—it's not your priority.

Start putting first things first. Spend time on whatever your top career and life priorities are first thing in the morning. Do what's most important when your brain is at its best. Before your willpower units are used up. Then do the second most important thing. Then the third most important thing. And so on.

Unproductive people always avoid the most difficult task of the day. If you want to start being more productive, start doing the thing you dread the most first.

Some tasks have very high activation energies. They take extra willpower units to start. Cold calling potential clients. Having a difficult discussion with your boss or spouse. Renewing your license at the DMV before work. The only way to get these tasks done without waiting until the last minute is to do them first.

Do the most important activity of the day right when your mental energy is peaking. Don't save the hardest things for last. Don't cherry pick easy tasks off of your action items just to get a quick dopamine hit.

Choose the item you want to do the least and execute it in full force. Start your day where it hurts. It will make the rest of your day more pleasant and more productive overall.

Are You Living Your Life Eight Distracted Hours at a Time?

Eight-hour work days are an artifact of the Industrial Revolution.

They were invented to optimize assembly lines and manufacturing equipment run times; human happiness and success had nothing to do with it. Remember, you only get about 90–120 minutes of peak mental energy and five hours or less of near peak mental energy each day.

That's it. As a result, your goal each day should be to work hard for five hours and then coast.

Everything you do after five hours of working is average at best. After the first five hours of the work day, your brain is running on about half of its mental energy. As a result, how productive you are in life comes down to what you consistently do during the first few hours of the work day.

Start making those hours count.

Unproductive people love to look at their phone all day. They love to open their Gmail or Messenger app to quickly skim their emails and texts for any golden nuggets that will give their brain a quick dopamine hit. These people are just like gamblers in Vegas pumping dollars into slot machines waiting for the next mediocre payout.

Except, in this case, you're pumping out something much more valuable than dollar bills; you're pumping out your mental energy. If you want to be more productive, start refusing to look at your phone before lunch. There's nothing important on your phone. It's just a distraction.

Every ring, beep, and alert you see or hear is one less willpower unit you have for that day. Turn off your alerts. Delete your games. If you're in sales or trade stock and have to use your phone during normal working hours, wake up earlier.

Start your five hours of undistracted work before the calls start coming in. Line up the calls you want to make before you start getting pushed around by the calls other people make. Set your own agenda. Don't stay at the mercy of other people's agenda. At the very least, schedule set times during the day for when you will make and take calls, and when you will use your phone in general.

The same holds true for your email inbox. If you want to start being more productive, start only checking your email during set times during the day. Your inbox is not your to-do list. It's other people's to-do list. The more emails you answer, the more you're working for others and not for yourself.

Stop answering emails just to feel busy, significant, and connected.

Most importantly, *stop answering emails right away*. Every time you respond to an email right away, you're communicating that your attention is easily obtained. How busy can you be if you volley an email immediately back at a colleague or potential investor?

Plus, you're training people to expect a quick response. This makes it impossible to *over-deliver* down the road. It's like cleaning your room every day without your parents asking. They'll start to expect it. They'll stop being happy about it. Instead, they'll get mad when you don't do it every day.

A better strategy is to clean your room after you've been asked more than once. Then cleaning it is never *expected*. Now, when you finally do clean your room, your parents are really happy and thank you for it. By only working through your inbox once or twice a day, you help people understand that you *are not* immediately available.

This gives you room to breathe.

It gives you room to get real work done.

This also prevents you from getting caught in a flurry of mentally draining emails at any given hour of the day. You also avoid the dreaded two-second later response that makes you feel like you have to answer immediately because the other party knows you just sent an email. There are no email emergencies. If there's really an emergency, they'll call. Or, they'll come to your office. Or, they'll wait.

The most significant productivity pitfall to avoid is readily accepting other people's favor requests. If you want to start being more productive, you must start making people ask you for favors three times before accepting. You'll never be happy in life if answering "yes" is your default. Recall that answering "yes" to everything is the fast track to productivity failure.

One string of misguided "yeses" will spread you so thin that your entire career and reputation collapses. One misguided string of agreements can put your home life into a tailspin for weeks or months. Start saying "no." Unless someone is literally about to die, say "no" first. You cannot master the art of pragmatic thinking without setting "no" as your default state.

Case Study #5: Catherine Sorbara, PhD

From stress and depression to Antarctica and the C-suite

In the final stages of her graduate school career, Catherine Sorbara was living in Germany and working to complete the last experiments for a manuscript that needed to be submitted the day before.

Oh, and she was also planning her wedding.

Like most graduate students in their final year, she was working twelve hours a day in the lab and then going home to write her thesis. She would work all day, write all night, and then wake up the next morning after five hours of sleep and do the same thing all over again.

Eventually, Cathy defended her thesis and received her degree. She published well and graduated summa cum laude. On paper, everything was perfect. But in real life, something wasn't quite right. Cathy was suffering.

Cathy felt guilty about everything. She felt like she was not performing high enough, not achieving better results, not working long enough. Cathy's self-worth was at an all-time low. She was depressed and in pain. But this wasn't new for Cathy. She had been receiving psychotherapy and taking medication for depression for over two years now.

When Cathy first read that two-thirds of academics suffer mental health problems that they attribute to their work situation, she couldn't believe it. But then, in the months leading up to end of her PhD career, Cathy began to feel overwhelmed with fear and anxiety.

Most other graduate students in her situation were searching for possible postdoctoral positions and were filled with excitement now that the light at the end of the tunnel was becoming brighter.

Cathy was not one of these students.

She had no idea what she wanted to do, and it scared her.

Could she have spent over 20 years of her life training for something she didn't want to do anymore? This fear paralyzed Cathy and, as a result, she did not apply for any positions.

When she finished her PhD, she ended up unemployed, which created even more stress.

Cathy needed something to do; she needed problems to solve. So, she started inventing them. Cathy began creating drama with her husband just to have something to engage her. She would obsess over what was going on in her circle of friends and community: who said what? What's happening when? She didn't want to miss out on anything.

Cathy knew what she was doing though. She knew what kind of person this drama and gossip and meaninglessness was turning her into, and that made her even more depressed—even a little bitter.

One day Cathy decided that enough was enough. She realized that no one was coming to save her. She was going to have to save herself. She still felt pain, but she felt energized, too. Energy she could use.

The problem was she was focusing on the wrong things—drama, gossip, missing out, etc. Cathy was filling the void in her life with nonsense.

While earning her PhD, Cathy had wished for the moment when she could have more time to do the things she wanted to do. After graduation, that moment arrived, but she didn't know how to handle it. Hence the downward spiral. Now, she realized that it was up to her to make the most of her PhD, her career, and her overall life.

Cathy threw herself headfirst into writing a blog, volunteering for a women in science group, and her job search. She turned her pain into productivity, and within a month she had a job as a publishing editor for the Royal Society of Chemistry. Within a year, she was in a C-Suite position as Chief Operations Officer at Cheeky Scientist, a company that specializes in career development for PhDs.

During this time, Cathy created a non-negotiable: she would never let her work come before her mental and emotional health. Cathy has since traveled the world many times over and was chosen as one of only 80 women in STEM (Science Technology Engineering & Math) globally to travel to Antarctica as part of an initiative to heighten the voice of women leaders and shape global policy.

Note

1. 'Reciprocity'. Wikipedia: https://en.wikipedia.org/wiki/Reciprocity_(social_psychology)

30 Is Everyone a Narcissist Now?

The problem with labels is that they lead to stereotypes and stereotypes lead to generalizations and generalizations lead to assumptions and assumptions lead back to stereotypes.

—Ellen DeGeneres

I was in a very serious relationship a few years ago. I had worked really hard to become a priority in her life. We hit our stride for a few years, and life was great. Then we started having problems. Nothing big at first, just the usual little problems that creep up.

But the problems got bigger. Our paths started to diverge.

We started having ugly arguments. She would threaten to leave. I would threaten to leave. We entered this awkward "push–pull" period of trying to convince each other to stay and then pushing each other to go. This back-and-forth went on for months.

There was a stretch of time within those months that I tried my hardest to fix the relationship. I tried to get things back to the honeymoon phase. I tried to turn back time. But the more I tried, the less she seemed to try. The more I made her a priority, the less she prioritized me.

To be fair, the reverse of this occurred at times too. I remember thinking during these times that she was so selfish. She was so obsessed with herself. She was such a narcissist.

The truth was, she just wasn't into me anymore. I wasn't a priority to her, and that was her decision to make. Once I stopped blaming her and labeling her, things got better. Once I took responsibility for myself and took action to better my situation, my life improved.

Narcissism is a Buzzword for Self-Pity

Your ex-relationship partner is not a narcissist. At least, the odds are against it. The *Journal of Clinical Psychiatry* published a very large-scale, peer-reviewed scientific study of 34,653 adults and found that the prevalence of ever experiencing Narcissistic Personality Disorder was only 6.2%.[1] Only 6.2% over the course of a lifetime.

That means that my ex is likely not a narcissist. Instead, I was just replacing my feelings of sadness and anger with a false label. I was taking the easy road by calling someone a name instead of doing the hard work of taking responsibility for myself and taking action to change my life.

Calling other people names might make you feel better about the fact that you're no longer a priority to them, but it's not going to make your situation any better in the real world.

A better strategy is to take action to remove these people from your life. If you've made someone else a priority and they've refused to do the same, get surgical. Cut them out of your life.

Don't call ten friends and whine about it. Don't complain and research personality disorders online. Instead, take action to get them out of your space.

Before labeling others as negative, manipulative, or narcissistic, first ask yourself: "How can I take responsibility for myself?" "How can I change the situation with my actions, not label people with my words?"

Once you've asked these questions, take the following two steps.

First, quit seeking a confession of wrongdoing from the person who hurt you, or from anyone ever.

Any time you spend trying to hold up a mirror to show someone they're wrong is a complete waste of time. It's a waste of time because no one will ever see themselves as a bad person. Sure, they might see that they've made a mistake. They might see that they've hurt you.

But they'll never see that they unjustly hurt you. They'll never see themselves as inherently unjust or evil. Most importantly, even if they see it, they'll never admit to it. So let it go and quit wasting your time trying to get a confession.

Besides, what's on the other end of a confession? A few good feelings? Sure, you might feel good that you won an argument or got someone to confess to something, but these feelings are not going to bring you any closer to improving your life. Instead, your whining and complaining are going to create more obstacles for you.

Second, learn to expect less from other people and more from yourself. Most of the pain you will ever experience in life is due to your own mismanaged expectations. Of course, it's going to hurt when you expect people to give you the world and they don't deliver. Stop expecting other people to live and die for you.

Stop expecting others to fix whatever is broken in your life. This just isn't practical. You're not the center of anyone's universe. If you want something done, look to yourself to do it. If you want to feel better, look to yourself to improve. Quit waiting for some fairy godmother to drop into your lap and solve all your problems. No one is coming to help you get over heartache or any other problems in your life. You're going to have to be pragmatic and help yourself grow.

Note

1. Stinson, F.S., *et al*. (2008). 'Prevalence, correlates, disability, and comorbidity of DSM-IV narcissistic personality disorder: results from the wave 2 national epidemiologic survey on alcohol and related conditions'. *Journal of Clinical Psychiatry*. *69*(7):1033–45. https://www.ncbi.nlm.nih.gov/pubmed/18557663

31 Seeing Through the Victim Illusion

When you think everything is someone else's fault, you suffer a lot. When you realize that everything springs only from yourself, you will learn both peace and joy.

—Dalai Lama

I laid face down on the cold, hard table with my shirt off. Ten people were circled around me. I could feel the pressure of the gun against my lower back. There's something about having your first health crisis that makes you question the world. It makes you question yourself too.

A handful of specialists recently told me that I needed a kidney biopsy. "You need a kidney biopsy" is a nice way of saying you're about to be shot in the back with a tiny gun that's going to reach inside of you and pull out a chunk of your internal organs.

There I was—shirtless and face down with a biopsy gun against my back. Terrified. The results came back positive for a stress-induced kidney condition. The next few months were awful. I slunk around at work and home telling people about what I was going through.

I had a lot of sympathetic phone conversations with people who really cared and told me that everything was going to be okay. These conversations were meaningful and helpful ... for a while.

Then they became a crutch. I felt sorry for myself for so long and had so many sad conversations that I started getting angry when other people didn't feel sorry for me. I started expecting people to treat me like a victim.

After all, I deserved it. I was a victim. I didn't do anything to earn this condition—to have to go through dozens of painful and scary medical procedures. I didn't ask for this. Poor me.

A few people told me to buck up and get back to living my normal life. I hated them for it. "How dare you!" I thought. "You have no idea what I'm going through." "Pity me. Treat me like I'm special. Do what I say and what I want because I'm in emotional pain."

It seems pathetic and shameful now, but these are the actual thoughts that went through my head. Finally, months later, I realized that my victim mentality wasn't making me stronger. It was making me weaker. It was slowly eroding my self-esteem, relationships, and life.

How to Deal With People Who Play the Victim (Yourself Included)

You must guard yourself against playing the victim, and you must not allow others to play the victim with you.

In life, everyone is the victim of something, but not everyone chooses to behave with a victim mentality. Those who do decide to be a victim, end up living angrier, more selfish, and more entitled lives than those who refuse that mindset.

A Stanford University study reported in the *Journal of Personality and Social Psychology* found that playing the victim leads to a sense of entitlement and selfish behavior.[1] In one experiment, participants who were asked to remember a time when their lives were unfair were more likely to refuse to help someone complete a simple task than participants who were asked to recall a time when they were bored.

The same paper went on to review a collection of studies showing that all the things that make someone feel wronged, including disrespect, unequal treatment, disproportional income, diagnosis of a disease, and an unhappy childhood, make people feel more entitled to special treatment.

If someone starts playing the victim in your life, act quickly to diffuse the situation. Listen to their problems—*once*.

Let them get it all out and externalize what just happened to them. It will help them process the situation.

Then, when they're ready, turn their mental energy toward solutions. Work with them to create a positive vision for their future. Help them focus on what they're going to do, not what they're going through.

However, whatever you do, don't empower their feelings of self-victimization. Don't feed their problems with attention. Let them externalize once, then cut them off.

Have a zero tolerance policy for self-pity.

Of course, there are people with clinically diagnosed depression and other kinds of severe mental problems. Get these people the help they need. I'm talking about your friend who gets dumped and blames all of their problems on a "narcissistic" ex; your colleague who gets fired and complains about the bad economy or their "wrongful termination" instead of looking for a new job; your relative who gets a difficult diagnosis and lies around all day giving up on life. Don't allow these people to play the victim.

Instead, take your friend out to meet some new people, help your colleague update their résumé or create a business plan, and go on a walk with your relative.

The hardest part of dealing with those who play the victim is the social pressure you'll feel to let them do it. You've been raised by society to encourage this kind of behavior.

You've been told that letting people escape responsibility for overcoming the horrible things that can happen in life is a virtue. This lie ends here for you. From now on, when someone you know starts playing the victim, you'll know exactly how to handle it. You'll know how to either pull people who've become toxic victims back from the dark side, or how to cut them out of your life completely.

Note

1. Zitek, E., *et al.* (2010) 'Victim entitlement to behave selfishly'. *Journal of Personality and Social Psychology*, 98(2): 245–255. https://www.ncbi.nlm.nih.gov/pubmed/20085398

32 How Decision Fatigue Reduces Willpower

Human will-power alone is not enough. Will-power is excellent and we should always be using it; but it is not enough. A desire to live a good life is not enough. Obviously we should all have that desire, but it will not guarantee success.

—David Lloyd-Jones

Remember when you were a kid and each day seemed to last forever? But then you got older. And the days grew shorter.

Now, months pass by like days and days fly by like minutes.

This happens because, as we grow older, we fill up our days with more and more decisions and planned activities. When you're a kid, you don't have any plans. You don't make difficult decisions. You wake up; someone feeds you, takes you places, takes care of you, and tells you what to do. The rest of your time is spent playing without an agenda. As a result, your days are endless, and your energy levels are limitless.

Compare that to now.

Studies show that the average adult can make up to 35,000 decisions a day.[1] Each of these decisions takes time and energy. Eventually, they start to pile up, weighing you down and locking you into place.

Decision fatigue refers to the deteriorating quality of decisions made by an individual after a long session of deliberation. Decision fatigue is also known as *ego depletion*, a term coined by the social psychologist Roy F. Baumeister. Baumeister's work has demonstrated that you have a finite store of mental energy for exerting self-control. When your stores are empty, your ability to make good decisions deteriorates.

One of Baumeister's studies divided college students into two different groups. The first group, labeled the Deciders, were told that they would get to keep a gift at the end of the experiment if they made a series of choices between the available options.

Would they prefer a pen or T-shirt? A red T-shirt or a black T-shirt? A candle or a T-shirt? A vanilla-scented candle or an almond-scented candle?

The second group, or Non-deciders, spent the same amount of time contemplating the same products but without making any choices. Instead, they were asked to give their opinions about the gifts.

After the questions, all of the participants were told to hold one of their hands in ice water for as long as they could (a classic test of self-control).

The biological impulse is to pull your hand out of the water, so self-discipline is needed to keep your hand submerged. The *Non-deciders* lasted an average of 67 seconds, while the *Deciders* lasted an average of only 28 seconds. Deciding between simple items that carried no significance made the students twice as weak.

How Are You Spending Your Decision-Making Units?

Your willpower consists of a set number of decision-making units. These units affect your ability not only to make good decisions but to focus and concentrate in general.

Whenever you make a decision, your willpower suffers. Think of willpower as a kind of instinctual override, a way to interrupt your brain's automatic processing to do something else.

If you're hungry and come upon a table of free doughnuts, the primitive part of your brain will process the event and say, "EAT!" But the more advanced decision-making part of your brain will tell you to keep walking and not take the bait. Willpower is simply your ability to inhibit your brain's natural inclinations. It's your ability to make good decisions.

A study published in the *Journal of Personality* shows that each person has his or her own individual willpower limit and this limit is depleted by mental strain.[2] Another study done at Stanford University shows exactly how this works. The experiment involved two groups of students—people in the first group were given a two-digit number to remember, while the second group was given a seven-digit number to remember.[3]

Both groups were instructed to remember the number, walk down a long hallway, and repeat the number to an administrator at the end of the hall. Halfway down the hall, a young woman waited by a table with a large plate of fresh fruit on one side and a large plate of pastries on the other side.

She asked each participant to choose which snack they would like to eat after completing the memorization task. The people in the second group, those laboring under the strain of remembering a seven-digit number, chose a pastry far more often than those who were remembering the two-digit number.

Your willpower is what allows you to make pragmatic decisions. The problem is that mental strain of any kind, including the pressure of making even simple, meaningless decisions, reduces your willpower. Studies show that the only way to restore your willpower is to eat more simple sugars, sleep, or stop actively making decisions. Assuming you want to avoid diabetes and you're already getting eight hours of quality sleep, the only strategy left for protecting your willpower is to reduce the number of decisions you make each day. But how is this possible when you want to improve your relationships, career, and overall life?

The answer lies in creating and stacking mini-habits.

Notes

1. Allen, J. (2012) 'Decisions, decisions … dopamine?' http://www
    .capitalcityweekly.com/stories/021512/new_955739899.shtml

2. Baumeister, R. (2006) 'Self-regulation and personality: How interventions increase regulatory success, and how depletion moderates the effects of traits on behavior'. *Journal of Personality.* *74*(6): 1773–1802. http://onlinelibrary.wiley.com/doi/10.1111/j.1467 –6494.2006.00428.x/abstract

3. Lehrer, J. (2009) 'Blame it on the brain: The latest neuroscience research suggests spreading resolutions out over time is the best approach'. *The Wall Street Journal.* https://www.wsj.com/articles/ SB10001424052748703478704574612052322122442

33 Hacking and Stacking Mini-Habits to Success

Your net worth to the world is usually determined by what remains after your bad habits are subtracted from your good ones.

—Benjamin Franklin

After my diagnosis and surgery, and after I learned how to channel my pain and stress into growth, I relied heavily on the power of habit to create lasting changes in my life.

To be honest, my motivation to make a particular change never lasted longer than the decision to make it.

I want to start eating more green vegetables and juicing vegetables to drink, too. *Sounds like a good idea, Isaiah. Let's do it.*

I'm tired and want to eat four bacon-double-cheese hamburgers. *Sure thing, Isaiah. Screw all that juicing stuff.*

That's how all my good decisions to change ended up when I relied exclusively on staying motivated to follow through with them.

Motivation, usually in the form of pain, can come and go like the wind. Habits, on the other hand, are like the fitted metal wheels of a freight train. They plow through obstacles, take immense energy to slow down, and only move in one direction: forward.

Imagine that your habits are, in fact, the wheels on a very long freight train. How did they get there? Was the train held upside down by some invisible hand while all the wheels were snapped onto it simultaneously? Or, were the wheels carefully fastened onto the train one by one and then tightened, tested, and tightened again?

The latter, of course, is the answer.

Once I started relying on habits, in particular, mini-habits, to help me follow through on my good decisions, my life dramatically changed for the better.

Instead of making a big decision to renew my relationships, get back in shape, eat healthier, start juicing, go to church, volunteer, get a business mentor, take a finance and accounting course, learn to fly a Cirrus airplane, enter a new career, and begin writing this book all at once, I started small.

First, I dedicated a set amount of time each month to spend with the people who are important to me. Once this became a habit—a mini-habit—I scaled it up by dedicating time to my important relationships each week, and then each day, not just each month.

Next, I started going to the gym once a week and doing just two different exercises. Once this became a habit, I scaled up by going to the gym twice a week, then three times a week, then three times a week doing five different exercises.

On and on this went until I had made every single change I wanted to make. How long did it take to execute all of these changes using the mini-habit process? Three months. That's it.

By three months, all of my new habits were in motion, and every change had been made.

By six months, all of my new habits had come together and aligned to create a completely new lifestyle.

By nine months, I was a completely new person living a completely different life. This is the power of the mini-habit process.

A major factor to the success of this process was being very gentle with myself. If I made a mistake and broke one of my new habits as it was forming, I let it go. I did not allow myself to feel guilty and I refused to beat myself up internally. Instead, I'd just adjust course to get back on track.

Returning to the freight train metaphor, the wheels on any given train turn very little on their own. Instead, it's the railroad track's job to gently guide the wheels to the left or the right. There are never any sharp, right-angle turns on a railroad track, only very smooth, very gentle curves.

This is how you must learn to be with yourself—strong in your habits, so you're always moving forward, but forgiving of your mistakes so you can adjust and return to your course as needed.

The Habitual Mouse Gets the Cheese

During a series of experiments aimed at determining how habits work, researchers at MIT surgically placed wires and probes inside the brains of healthy mice and dropped them into a maze.[1]

Then, the researchers monitored the mice's brain activity as they navigated their way through the maze. During the first maze run, the mice's brain activity was very high, especially in the cerebral cortex. Yet, the mice went through the maze very slowly. They had to scratch and sniff the walls to find their way to the cheese at the end of the maze. Over the next few weeks, the mice found their way through the maze faster and faster. At the same time, something interesting happened: the mice's brain activity went down.

The researchers found that as the mice turned finding the cheese into a habit, their cerebral cortexes, including the parts associated with memory, became nearly silent. In other words, the mice were finding the cheese faster but using far less mental energy.

The only part of the mice's brain that was still active was a tiny part called the basal ganglia (the brain's habit center). The researchers concluded that the mice's brains had off-loaded the maze-running sequence from the cerebral cortex to the basal ganglia and stored it as a habit.

The researchers also made two other interesting discoveries. First, they were able to activate the mice's basal ganglia to run the maze-running script using a "click" sound as a trigger. Second, they were able to reactivate the mice's cerebral cortex by changing the maze or by moving the cheese.

Hacking and Stacking Mini-Habits

A full habit consists of a trigger, a routine, and a reward. In the above MIT experiments, the trigger was a "click" sound, the routine was the maze-running script, and the reward was the cheese.

A more practical example of a habit loop would be getting in your car after work and driving home. You've probably noticed that if you drive the same route home from work over and over again for months and months you will start to do it automatically.

In this scenario, the trigger would be getting off work, the routine would be the route you take, and the reward would be arriving home successfully. After driving this way repeatedly, your brain activity goes down. The routine gets off-loaded from your cerebral cortex to your basal ganglia.

That is why you can drive home and not really remember the time you spent driving—because your habit was in control of your decisions. The rest of your brain engages only when something new gets added to the routine, like road construction or a swerving car.

A mini-habit is just like a full habit except the routine is much smaller, or is merely a portion of a whole routine.

For example, if a full habit is flossing all of your teeth before bed. A mini-habit is flossing just one tooth. If a full habit is going to the gym after work to perform 30 sets of exercises, a mini-habit is going to the gym to do just one set of exercises.

Studies show that mini-habits are not only easier to create and follow, but can quickly lead to full habits. The trick is to grow your mini-habits into full habits slowly. After a few days of flossing one tooth, floss two teeth, then three, then your top teeth, and then all your teeth. After a few one-set exercise sessions, move up to two sets, then four sets, then eight, and so on.

Mini-habits are very scalable.

You can turn one mini-habit into a dozen full habits by stacking routines on top of each other.

The key is to use a really strong trigger, backed by a long-standing routine, to trigger a second routine. Then, use this second routine to trigger a third routine, on and on, until you have a long chain of routines that lead to a reward.

The strongest trigger I've been able to find in my life is the simple act of waking up. As long as I'm alive, this trigger will exist. And, for as long as I can remember, I've been brushing my teeth right after waking up.

A strong trigger backed by a long-standing routine is the ideal foundation for a new habit. When I wanted to start working out on a daily basis, I stacked the habit of exercising (which began as a one-set mini-routine and slowly grew into a 30-set workout) on top of the routine of waking up and brushing my teeth.

When I wanted to start eating a healthy breakfast every morning, I stacked the new habit of eating a healthy breakfast (which started as eating one piece of kale with my eggs and grew into eating a full plate of kale) on top of waking up, brushing my teeth, and working out.

When I wanted to start writing this book, I stacked the routine of writing for five minutes (which grew into writing for two hours) on top of my routine of waking up, brushing my teeth, working out, and eating a healthy breakfast.

My morning habit has continued to scale to include over fifteen different routines, each acting as a trigger for the next. Consequently, I don't make a single decision from about 6 a.m. to 1 p.m. each day. This keeps my schedule open, my mind free, and my energy levels high (the reward).

Turn Deliberate Action into a Habit

Let your environment make decisions for you. It is better to make a bold decision, choose poorly, learn from it immediately, and take action to correct it than it is to deliberate obsessively, sap all of your energy, choose correctly, and have no time or energy to follow through on your choice.

Your goal is to identify the pragmatic actions that further your greater purpose in life and turn them into habits as quickly as possible.

The best way to do this is by favoring action over planning.

Plans involve decisions. The more you plan, the weaker your mind becomes. Action, on the other hand, will make your decisions for you. Your actions will either bring you closer to your goal or take you further from it. You can use this feedback to identify the productive actions and turn them into stackable habits.

Of course, you will never be completely free from the responsibility of making good choices. But you can free yourself from decision fatigue and feeling trapped in your own life. And, in turn, you can extend your ability to make important decisions pragmatically.

The more healthy habits you stack on top of each other, the fewer unimportant decisions you will have to make. As a result, you will free up your time and energy for the things that matter, like having adventures and indulging in the people and projects you've been putting off.

Case Study #6: Jamie Johnston, R.M.T.

"It's a happy ending, but don't call it that."

Jamie Johnston was a fireman, first-aid instructor, a professional hockey trainer, and a registered massage therapist.

You could also add that he was a workaholic.

But no matter how hard Jamie worked, he could never get ahead. His bills piled up and his work days got longer and longer until Jamie started to feel like there was no point in working hard, like everything he was told about hard work paying off was a lie.

Things were bad, and then they got worse.

Jamie's financial troubles continued, and he ended up having to declare bankruptcy. During this time, Jamie developed severe sleep apnea. He went nearly a year without sleeping through the night. At one point, he went to a sleep clinic, and after the clinicians had monitored him, they were amazed that he was able to remember anything at all.

Jamie wasn't getting any REM sleep, the deep, "Rapid Eye Movement" sleep required for consolidating memories, thanks to all the stress keeping him up at night.

Jamie found himself broke, juggling multiple jobs, and unable to relax, let alone fall asleep. His willpower was shattered at the end of every day, and as a result, he ate fast food and drank alcohol every night. Jamie knew he had to make a change.

The problem, Jamie realized, boiled down to his habits. He was working hard, but he wasn't working smart. Jamie wasn't focused, and he wasn't organized. His life had no routine, no structure. Jamie woke up every day scrambling, not knowing which job he'd be going to or what he had to accomplish for the day. But instead of leveraging healthy habits to keep his maxed out life from spinning out of control, he did nothing.

Why did Jamie refuse to change? It was simple: he felt like a victim.

After all, hadn't he done his part? Jamie had worked hard, and now life owed him. He had four jobs for crying out loud! He deserved happiness and success! He deserved peace!

Finally, after a near mental breakdown, Jamie realized that the only thing keeping him from living the life he wanted was himself. So, he called all of his jobs and took an entire weekend off—something he had not done for over five years.

That weekend, Jamie slept.

When Jamie woke up, he sat down with me to create a strategic plan for the lifestyle he wanted to live.

First, Jamie took a leave of absence from three of his jobs. Next, he created a morning routine that he would follow religiously moving forward. This routine lasted from when he woke up until 12 noon every day, during which he accomplished all of his most important tasks for the day without having to make a single decision on what to do between tasks.

The routine quickly became a habit that Jamie followed automatically. After a week, Jamie had more hours of free time than he knew what to do with. So, he started building a platform that would help registered massage therapists keep up with their training, while also ensuring they kept up with best practices in first aid and small business management.

Within six months, Jamie's The Massage Therapy Development Center (TheMTDC) became one of the most highly trafficked training platforms for registered massage therapists in the world.

Note

1. Duhigg, C. (2012) *The Power of Habit: Why we do what we do, and how to change*. London: William Heinemann.

34 Leveraging Boredom and Filling the Mental Void

One of the drawbacks about adventures is that when you come to the most beautiful places you are often too anxious and hurried to appreciate them.

—C.S. Lewis

If you've come this far, your mind is free. That is to say, you've learned how to be selective with your focus, how to be a creative owner, and how to grow pragmatically. This is where a lot of people stumble.

The reason they stumble is simple: improvement comes at a price.

The price is boredom. Or at least a propensity to be bored.

When you've cut out all of the energy-sucking drama and dependency in your life and put all the nagging parts of your life on autopilot, there will be a void. At first, this void will be pleasant and invigorating. You'll relax. You'll wake up present and free of distractions.

Over time, however, this void can start to weigh on you. Human beings were not meant to be idle. Studies show that our happiness and health rely on constant movement, challenge, and growth. We are built for adventure.

Boredom in itself is not your enemy. In fact, boredom can make you more creative and adventurous.

If you're feeling the weight of the void you've created, you're primed for a breakthrough. Too many people think that boredom is the enemy of change. They think that boredom and breakthroughs are opposites. In reality, boredom is a springboard for innovation.

Boredom creates breakthroughs. A study reported in the *Creativity Research Journal* showed that engaging in boring, monotonous activities makes people more creative afterward.[1] As part of the study, 80 participants were asked to either copy numbers from a phonebook or not (control group), followed by an exercise to think of as many possible uses for a pair of plastic cups.

The group who had suffered through the boring phonebook task thought of more creative uses for the cups afterward. Other studies reported in the *Journal of Experimental Social Psychology* found that participants on creativity tests who were bored outperformed those who were relaxed, elated, or distressed.[2] The key is that boredom is an *approach* state. It drives action.

When leveraged correctly, boredom can spark change and help you improve your life for the better.

Using Boredom to Build a More Creative Future

You must leverage your boredom productively to become more successful.

Don't fall into the trap of cleaning up your life and conserving your mental energy only to get bored and crave stimulus so much that you start to manufacture drama.

Don't start to hunger for stimulus so much that you let other people suck you into their dramas. Don't start wasting your time surfing the internet without purpose or watching eight hours of TV.

Instead, get creative about what's possible for your future. The reason your life is so boring is that your thoughts have become boring. When you were a kid, your mind moved a mile per minute.

You had big dreams for your future. You wanted to be an astronaut, inventor, beauty queen, pro athlete, or a koala bear.

Whatever the biggest and the best thing you could imagine was—that's what you wanted to be.

Now, you want to be promoted to middle manager for some faceless company so you can get paid one more dollar an hour. Seriously, that's the big future most people are dreaming for in their lives.

They've given up on achieving greatness. They've given up on writing a book or starting a business. Instead, these people obsess over the most banal achievements imaginable.

A promotion at work. A two-week vacation. A good parking spot. Snore. No wonder everyone is bored out of their minds.

You did not read this entire book and spend countless hours organizing and automating your life so that you could keep going to work at the same position and keep living the same life.

You reached for high levels of *Intelligent Achievement* for a reason: to have an adventure. To be an adventurer. This means getting your passion for life back. It means opening your mind to what's possible for you.

You need to disassemble any limiting beliefs that have built up in your mind over the last few years. Stop selling yourself short and start realizing anything is possible. You could quit your job, walk away from everyone you know, move to Alaska, and join a fishing boat crew.

You could sell everything you own, lock yourself in a basement and write jokes for two weeks, buy a used car, and start your career as a country-touring standup comedian.

You could write a proposal and walk into your boss's office next week and ask to be transferred to a new department (one that you're going to create and manage). You don't have to do these things, but you do have to recognize that they're possible.

The reason you haven't left everything behind and reinvented yourself is not because you can't, it's because you won't. You've simply *chosen* to stay where you are. You've limited yourself by nothing more than your own mindset.

Anything is possible once you take responsibility for your own life. You are where you are because of you, not because of anyone else. You built the life you have right now, and you can make a new life at any time.

Channel your feelings of boredom and routine into a new, creative vision for your future. Connect possibilities wildly in your head and then write these connections down on paper. From there—refine, refine, and refine until you have a detailed picture of the passionate, adventurous life you want to live.

Filling the Void with Vitality and Adventure

Your mental energy links to your physical energy. Without it, your mind will suffer. Investing in yourself and pursuing high levels of *Intelligent Achievement* is not an end game.

It's a continuous process. Which means that you must stay healthy enough to support this process. Too many people reach a certain level of success in their life, become bored, give into the void, and then lose their vitality.

They become weak, sluggish, and perpetually sleepy.

Think about how active you were when you were younger. You didn't have a car, so you walked or rode your bike everywhere. Your attention span was non-existent, so you ran around in a fit of discovery 24/7. You were so interested in everything that you couldn't sit still for more than five minutes.

This is robust and vivacious living. But now, your standards have changed. You've grown up. You've accumulated deadlines and obligations. You have to make ends meet. All of this adult living has altered your perception of vitality.

Now, walking to the store or picking up your kid and throwing him into the air is working out. Now, sitting at your desk for 6 hours instead of 8 hours a day is healthy living. Now, eating a box of gluten-free cereal right before bed is eating like a champion. What happened?

First, you lost your perception. Then, you lost your vitality. Finally, you lost your passion. The only way to regain your passion is to realize that you're far lazier now than you used to be. It's time to get moving.

Mobility is the key to happiness and success. Mobility is the key to staying positive in negative situations. The more mobile you are, the more vivacious you are, and the more passionate and creative you are.

Motion creates emotion. Start moving. Start exuding. Start injecting your words with energy. Start projecting vitality, charisma, and enthusiasm into everything you do.

Cutting negative people, negative energy, and time-wasting tasks out of your life are not enough. You must now use your energy to create positive experiences and emotions. You must use it to produce.

Once you realize that boredom is a gift and once you recover your vitality, it's time to start having more adventures.

Adventure is your best investment. Adventure is the best reward for *Intelligent Achievement*. Jon Levy, a behavioral scientist and author of *The 2AM Principle*, demonstrates that an experience requires three things to be adventurous.

First, the experience must be remarkable—worth talking about. Second, it must involve adversity or perceived risk.

Third and finally, it must bring about growth. You must be a different person at the end of the experience.

Adventures, not possessions or praise, make people truly happy.

The only way to be more adventurous is to be more flexible. You need to stop being so rigid in how you can achieve your goals. Your goals in life should be firm, but your path to your goals should be adaptable.

Too many people today get stuck in ruts that they create for themselves. They wrongly imagine that there is only one way to do something and then go about doing the same things over and over and over again. They try and try but nothing changes.

Most people simply can't stomach being flexible. They stay rigid because rigidity is comfortable. As counter-intuitive as it seems, to them, rigidity is relaxing.

Rigidity is relaxing because it's secure.

When things are rigid, nothing changes. There are no surprises. Rigidity maintains the status quo and keeps everybody happy. Good for you—you're doing what we do. Good for you—you're not rocking the boat. Good for you—you're not making us look bad.

This is what everyone around you thinks when you stay rigid. They love you for it, and you love their approval. The only way to get your passion back and start living a more adventurous life is to break these chains of approval.

Stop being so rigid and start being flexible. Start shaking things up. Start having adventures.

An adventure is an unusually exciting and risky experience. This is what you should be chasing now—unusual, exciting, and risky experiences, not approval.

Notes

1. Mann, S. and R. Cadman. (2014). 'Does being bored make us more creative?' *Creativity Research Journal* 26(2): 165–173. http://www.tandfonline.com/doi/abs/10.1080/10400419.2014.901073#.VcUdexNVikp

2. Gasper, K. and B. Middlewood. (2014). 'Approaching novel thoughts: Understanding why elation and boredom promote associative thought more than distress and relaxation'. *Journal of Experimental Social Psychology* 52: 50–57. http://www.sciencedirect.com/science/article/pii/S0022103113002205

CONCLUSION: A PRACTICAL GUIDE TO INTELLIGENT ADVENTURE

It's a magical world, Hobbes, ol' buddy ... Let's go exploring.
—Calvin from *Calvin and Hobbes* (Bill Watterson)

After mastering the principles of selectivity, ownership, and pragmatism in your life, you need to start reinvesting your newly found freedom in adventure. *Intelligent Achievement* and intelligent adventure go hand-in-hand.

Success, if done right, should lead you to increased levels of discovery, awe, and fun which, in turn, will make you more creative, more productive, and more successful.

The good news is that having an intelligent adventure is easier than you think. You don't have to go to Antarctica or New Zealand to have an adventure. You don't have to bungee jump, either.

Instead, you can do simple things where you are right now to fill your life with more adventure. Here's a list of ten things you can do to have an intelligent adventure right now:

1. **Build a fort** – Why do kids instinctively build forts in trees, under the stairs, and with pillows? When I was a kid, every time my parents left me with a babysitter, I would flip the couch upside down and build a fortress with couch cushion trapdoors. I used to see everything as a potential fort. I bet you did too.

Everyone wants their own space (with or without armed guards and an alligator moat). Studies show that this is normal and healthy.[1] Human beings are territorial by nature. Whether it's a master bathroom, a walk-in closet, a man cave, or the house of your dreams, building a fortress is an adventure worthy of your energy.

2. **Have a feast** – The communal feast is one of the world's most familiar rituals, dating back to antiquity and appearing across numerous cultures. Feasting involves the public consumption of an elaborate meal often accompanied by entertainment.

   Throughout history, the purpose of feasting includes paying debts, gaining allies, intimidating enemies, negotiating war and peace, and celebrating rites of passage.

   The earliest references to feasting include the Sumerian myth of the god Enki offering the goddess Inanna cake and beer (~3000 B.C.E.) and worshippers of the Shang dynasty in China offering their ancestors wine and fruit (~1700 B.C.E.).[2] Scholars agree that feasting is an adventure that connects people in a deep, meaningful, and primal way.[3]

3. **Lead a tribe** – Leadership is an adventure. But no one is coming to nominate you to lead them. The only way to turn yourself into a leader is to start something on your own, whether it's a club, a nonprofit, business, or tradition, and then rally people around it. This is harder than it sounds, but the rewards are extravagant. For example, recent studies show that leaders have a higher sense of control in their lives and, as a result, maintain lower levels of cortisol in their bodies, have fewer health scares, and live much longer than non-leaders.[4]

4. Find a rival – Drawing a line in the sand between you and another person, a group of people, or an idea can sharpen your mind and energize your body. Competition brings out the best in everyone involved. Studies show that competition is ingrained in human behavior and is an effective way to improve both performance and happiness.[5] As such, rivalry may be the healthiest adventure of all.

5. Chase – Animals in the wild chase their prey, not just to eat, but because they enjoy the hunt. The chase itself activates the brain's reward system. The same is true for human beings. We experience anticipatory joy, or pleasure derived from anticipating a desired outcome.[6] Studies by Brain Knutson at Stanford University show that just looking at a desired object activates neural signals associated with the release of dopamine (a neurotransmitter associated with motivation and pleasure).[7] Knutson's work suggests that we enjoy pursuing the objects of our desire just as much as we enjoy obtaining them.

6. Be chased – Everyone wants to be desired, sought after, and appreciated for their talents and skills. In fact, research shows that the desire to be appreciated (especially at work) is one of the strongest desires people have.[8] Whether it's a company pursuing you for a position or a person pursuing you for a date, it feels good to be wanted. Being pursued is an adventure. But how do you make other people want you? Simple: want them to want you without needing them to want you. It's that easy and that hard.

7. **Create something** – The desire to create is a primal urge, and the act of creation is adventurous.[9] It's why children stack blocks and build forts from a very young age. The problem is that most people stop creating after high school or college and, instead, just follow orders, repeat tasks, and regurgitate information. Make it a goal to create something new each week, even if it's just a journal entry or a simple drawing.

8. **Get unbalanced** – The results of a famous longevity study that tracked 1500 people for almost 100 years found that sacrificing work–life balance to accomplish goals and live up to one's potential helped individuals live longer.[10] Yes, you read that right. People who lived part of their life way out of balance to achieve something important lived longer than people who lived well-balanced lives. In fact, there wasn't a single exception to this rule in the study. Is there anything more adventurous than taking on a massive, worthy goal and giving everything to it? Check out *The Longevity Project* by doctors Howard Friedman and Leslie Martin.[11]

9. **Sleep outside** – Studies show that sleeping outdoors can restore healthy melatonin levels and repair circadian timing.[12,13] The colder temperatures and increased ventilation associated with sleeping outside are also better for your health. Camping in the great outdoors or simply having a sleepover in the backyard with your kids is another easy way to make your life more adventurous.

10. **Go on a pilgrimage** – For centuries, people from cultures all around the world have gone on pilgrimages. A pilgrimage is a journey or search for moral or spiritual

significance, usually accomplished by walking a great distance. In general, traveling to new places acts to expand your mind and change your perspective. You can do this on a large scale by traveling to another country on vacation or hiking a well-known route like America's Pacific Crest Trail or Spain's Camino de Santiago.

Alternatively, you can go on a small-scale pilgrimage by finding a local hiking trail to transverse on the weekend or by going for a 20-minute walk through your neighborhood or a nearby park every morning.

A morning walk can do more for most people than Prozac. Scientific studies show that walking in the morning lowers stress and even relieves pain.[14] Do not underestimate the power and sense of adventure that a simple walk can provide.

Notes

1. Richtel, M. (2012) 'And the walls came tumbling down, again: Lessons in the art of pillow fort construction'. *The Wall Street Journal*. http://www.nytimes.com/2012/04/19/garden/lessons-in-the-art-of-pillow-fort-construction.html?pagewanted=all&_r=0

2. 'Feasting: The archaeology and history of celebrating food'. https://www.thoughtco.com/feasting-archaeology-and-history-170940

3. Stromberg, P. G. (2009) 'The great feast: The mystery lurking behind our national feast'. *Psychology Today*. https://www.psychologytoday.com/blog/sex-drugs-and-boredom/200911/the-great-feast

4. Telos consulting. 'Want to be less stressed and live longer? Think like a leader'. http://www.teleosconsulting.com/2012/11/want-to-be-less-stressed-and-live-longer-think-like-a-leader/

5. Richtel, M. (2012) 'The competing views on competition'. *New York Times*. http://www.nytimes.com/2012/10/11/garden/the-role-of-competitiveness-in-raising-healthy-children.html

6. Seppälä, E. (2013) 'How desire fools us: The benefits and dangers of the chase'. *Psychology Today.* https://www.psychologytoday.com/blog/feeling-it/201308/how-desire-fools-us-the-benefits-and-dangers-the-chase

7. Knutson, B. 'Visualizing desire'. Stanford University. https://www.youtube.com/watch?v=CUK8D-kX0fE

8. Brooks, C. (2012) 'Recognizing employees is crucial to retention'. *Business News Daily.* http://www.businessnewsdaily.com/2350-employee-recognition-happiness.html

9. Gonathellis, O. '5 Ways to connect with your desire to create'. http://psychcentral.com/blog/archives/2013/02/28/5-ways-to-reconnect-with-your-desire-to-create/

10. Logan, D. (2011) 'Leadership advice that can help you live longer'. *CBS: Moneywatch.* http://www.cbsnews.com/news/leadership-advice-that-can-help-you-live-longer/

11. Friedman, H. S. and L. R. Martin. (2012). *The Longevity Project: Surprising discoveries for health and long life from the landmark eight-decade study.* New York: Plume.

12. Krans, B. (2013). 'The health benefits of sleeping under the stars'. http://www.healthline.com/health-news/mental-sleeping-outdoors-does-wonders-for-your-health-080213

13. 'Circadian rhythm'. Wikipedia. https://en.wikipedia.org/wiki/Circadian_rhythm

14. *Huffington Post.* (2013). 'Studies show that walking in the morning lowers stress and even relieves pain'. http://www.huffingtonpost.com/2013/04/03/national-walking-day-stress-relief-tips_n_2992972.html

EPILOGUE: LEGACY

No legacy is so rich as honesty.

—William Shakespeare

A legacy is something of value handed down from one generation to the next. Your legacy is what you will leave behind you when you die. Whether it's a child, a product, a service, a message, a way of doing things, or your own character, the time to start adding value to it is now.

If you want to leave a legacy, you must produce something so inspiring and valuable that it drives future generations to sustain it. This means that you must create something significant. And that means understanding the difference between significance and self-importance.

It is impossible to leave a legacy when you are absorbed in your own importance. Looking good and having power cannot be passed on.

When you die, anyone who listened to you because they feared you will not help you carry on your mission. Likewise, anyone whom you manipulated into amplifying your message will drop it once you're gone. The only things self-important people pass on are fables warning the next generation how *not* to live. Their lives are lessons, not legacies.

Most people yearn for a significant life. They want to know that their lives mattered. They want to know that they made a positive difference on this planet.

The problem is that many of these people transform their desire to live a significant life into a desire to be more important than their peers. Instead of focusing on adding value and developing as a leader, these people focus on looking good. Instead of creating and connecting, they consume and cut off. Self-important people equate their significance to their ability to show other people that they're right.

Forcing other people to see and do things your way is not significance. True significance can only be achieved through inspiration, and no one can be compelled to be inspired.

Free yourself from the tyranny of image. Instead of constructing an image of how you want other people to see you, start developing a reputation for being the kind of person you want to be.

Your reputation is a record of your achievement and reliability. It is both your personal profile and past performance history. Unlike images, your reputation doesn't fit you into a box. Reputations allow for mistakes. Reputations are constantly being rebuilt and improved.

This is because reputations move in one direction: forward. When you invest in your reputation over image, you don't have to fear the opinions of others. You don't have to put all your stock into looking good and enforcing your own opinions. Instead, you can focus on being your authentic self. Authenticity is inspiring.

It is also liberating. Mistakes can shatter an image, but not a reputation. Your reputation is a learning process. If you screw up, simply own up to it, learn from it, and move forward.

The most important and least important people in history have all ended up in the *same place*.

Everyone who has ever won an argument, lost an argument, proved someone wrong, was treated unfairly, hurt someone, or was hurt by someone, has ended up in this place.

Likewise, everyone who has ever started a feud, held a grudge, got away with something, or looked good in front of other people has ended up in this place too.

Where is this place?

The graveyard.

Your life on this earth will end one day.

You will never be more important or more powerful than Father Time. He sits across from you waiting, silently counting down as you spend your energy protecting your image, engaging in battles that don't matter, and chasing fake success.

You only have one opportunity to leave your mark. You only have one moment to seize your destiny. You can't chase fake success and *Intelligent Achievement* at the same time. You have to choose one or the other, and time is running out.

Choose wisely.

BONUS: ACHIEVING ALIGNMENT

Happiness is when what you think, what you say, and what you do are in harmony.

—Mahatma Gandhi

Have you ever tried solving a Rubik's Cube?

If you're like most people, you've played with this six-sided puzzle from the 1980s but never got around to solving it. The truth is, solving a Rubik's Cube is easy—if you use the right system.

The best method for solving the puzzle is to set one block of any color in the center of one side of the cube and keep it there. This is your focal point. From there, the goal is to manipulate and reorder that same side of the cube until every block matches the color of the block you set in the center.

To successfully solve the Rubik's Cube, repeat this sequence for all six sides of the cube.

Success in life is no different. No matter what you're trying to achieve, aligning your efforts is crucial to achieving accelerated returns. When it comes to *Intelligent Achievement*, you now know your efforts are best spent on selectivity, ownership, and pragmatism.

The final step is to align these three areas of your life towards a single point—a single purpose.

If you are interested in learning more about aligning your values and your goals to reach the pinnacle of *Intelligent Achievement* in your life, email me here:

mylifealigned@gmail.com

I will also send you the first step of "my revised and expanded *Escape Plan* program, as well as the first step of my new *Entrepreneur's Escape Plan* program, which shows you how to best align your values and efforts towards your personal and professional goals so you can reach the highest levels of *Intelligent Achievement*. As an additional bonus, I'll send you all the raw materials, case studies, and exercises for this book.

To *your success,*

—Isaiah

INDEX